Contents

Acknowledgments

The authors would like to thank Beth Cohen, LCSW, Josh Cantwell, LCSW, Lora Leslie, LCSW, Wendie Clemens, MA, LPC, Kerry Harlin, LCSW, Jeff Harlin, LCSW, and Emily and Aaron Crowell for reading various chapters and not being afraid to tell us what we were missing. Their feedback was incredibly valuable and needed. We also appreciate the time that Yvon Caselman spent doing the tedious job of checking references for us (and we hope that she is still speaking to us). We appreciate Caroline Walton at JKP for her patience in answering our endless questions and those who provided childcare for Kimberly. And, finally, we appreciate the hundreds of families we have worked with over the years. We have learned so much from them. Bless you for sharing your lives with us.

CHAPTER 1
Introduction

Evidence-Based Practice

Clients have a right to receive services that are proven to be successful. In fact, it is our ethical obligation as counselors to provide clients with the most effective available treatments. Because of this, there are increasing efforts in both medical and mental health communities to give priority to empirically based interventions (evidence-based practices). This, of course, requires practitioners to be well informed and up to date with knowledge of evidence-based practices. Practitioners must commit themselves to ongoing knowledge attainment through life-long learning.

The effectiveness of systemic (family) therapy is well established in the empirical literature. In a review of 20 meta-analyses, Shadish and Baldwin (2003) found that individuals with a range of mental health problems who were treated with couples or family therapy showed better outcomes than 71 percent of families who received standard services. Carr (2009a, 2009b) scrutinized these findings in more detail by singling out specific adult and child problems and examining meta-analyses, systematic literature reviews and controlled trials by problem area. His findings supported the effectiveness of family interventions over individual interventions for attachment problems, child abuse/neglect, behavioral problems, anxiety, depression, eating disorders and somatic problems in children; and for domestic violence, anxiety disorders, mood disorders, alcohol abuse, schizophrenia and adjustment to chronic illness in adults.

Indeed, empirical evidence affirms what family theories have said all along. Families are joined by strong emotional connections and individuals are strongly influenced by the dynamics and communication patterns of their families. Families are a "system" and often the most effective way to help an individual is to activate the family system and its resources. When a family member struggles with emotional problems, family work is not only an effective modality for improving relationships, but it is effective for the individual's emotional problems as well. Family work can open up avenues for progress that can be hard to discover in working with the individual only.

Family Types

Many modern families do not meet the definition of traditional, nuclear families. Families today have opposite-sex married parents, opposite-sex unmarried parents, single parents, same-sex parents, stepparents or extended family as parents. Couples of all ages live together without children and consider themselves families as well. Family structures themselves do not indicate the health of a family—they are simply the physical makeup of family members in relation to one another without respect to roles. It is important as counselors that we respect, accept and validate all types of families.

In addition to family structure, families are quite diverse based on race/ethnicity, culture, religion, beliefs/values, geographic location, immigration status and economic status. All of these elements of a family affect roles and behaviors in a family. For example, in the United States, ethnic minority groups are more strongly influenced by extended family, thereby changing the nature of family boundaries. Gay, lesbian, bisexual and transgendered families struggle with external oppression from community homophobia, thereby changing the ability to seek many external support systems.

Attendance in Family Sessions

Those participating in family therapy can include anyone who is involved in the situation or the presenting problem. Sometimes sessions include one or both parents alone; other times they include parent(s) and children together; and other times they may include some or all of the children without the parents. Grandparents, extended family members and even close family friends can be included in sessions if it is deemed to be helpful. It is up to the family and the counselor to decide together who should attend. What is vitally important is that participating family members are engaged and motivated.

Joining with the Family

It is essential that counselors join with each family member during initial sessions— that the family "buys into" participation. Research is very clear that the quality of the relationship between the counselor and the family is a strong indicator of families remaining in and improving in treatment (e.g. Miller and Rollnick 2002; Robbins *et al.* 2003). It is important for counselors to create a sense of collaboration with the family through empathy, positive regard and genuineness.

Joining is done by expressing interest in understanding each family member as an individual and in understanding the family as a whole. It is particularly important to join with and respect powerful family members. This is because they are the ones who have the power to take the family out of counseling. It is important not to confront those in power too early in the process of establishing a therapeutic relationship. It is also very important to join with any unlikable family member or the identified client.

A valuable aspect of joining with the family is "mimesis." This is a form of mimicking the family's language, gestures, tone, etc. in an effort to connect with them. For example, if the family is religious, it may be helpful to speak of God. If the family lives in a rural community, it may be helpful to speak of seasons, cycles, crops or animals. If the family is musical, it may be helpful to speak of harmony, tones and timing. Whatever language a family uses should be the language the counselor uses. In addition:

> A therapist…adopts the family's tempo of communication slowing his pace, for example, in a family that is accustomed to long pauses and slow responses. In a jovial family he becomes jovial and expansive. In a family with a restrictive style, his communication becomes sparse (Minuchin 1974).

General Guidelines

Relationships versus Individuals

Family work highlights interactions and relationship dynamics. Rather than focusing solely on an individual's thought processes, feelings and experiences, it seeks to understand and improve what happens *between* family members. Its emphasis is on communication, conflict resolution, power, flexibility, cohesion, roles, etc. It sees the family as a unit. It examines the dynamics between family members and not simply individual members' reactions or behaviors (Worden 2002). It seeks change through the interactions between family members rather than through individual intrapsychic work.

Process versus Content

In working with families, it is important to focus on patterns of interaction (process) rather than specific information or events (content). Content is the concrete topic being discussed (what is being said), whereas process refers to the interaction dynamics that underlie the content (Worden 2002). Rather than simply listening to the words that family members exchange, it is important to observe nonverbal communication, such as emotion, tone, body language, seating arrangements, who speaks to whom, etc. By focusing on the family process, counselors can identify underlying power relationships, family alliances, unresolved conflicts, etc. Its what the family does—not what they say—that is more poignant.

Linear versus Circular

Family therapists look at circular causality rather than linear causality. This means that events and behaviors are reciprocal in nature and often have multiple causes rather than just one cause. In its most simplistic form it suggests that *both* A's behavior is a result of B's behavior and B's behavior is a result of A's behavior. Each family member contributes to the behaviors and interactions of its members. There is not a single "cause" (Worden 2002). Therefore, the objective is not to find blame (where the problem started) because this can actually *amplify* the problem. Instead, causality is considered circular, which helps put the focus on finding solutions.

Counselor Reluctance to do Family Work

Despite the evidence that family work produces better and more sustained outcomes, many counselors are reluctant to do family work. They describe feelings of professional inadequacy and personal fears regarding emotionally charged sessions. They often justify their avoidance of family work by referring to a lack of education and experience. Indeed, many graduate programs offer minimal coursework in family work. And, it is true, family sessions can include escalated feelings, chaotic interactions and complex dynamics—sometimes appearing out of control—very different from individual counseling, where sessions are often predictable and simple.

The preference for working with individuals rather than families is also rooted in our many theories regarding individual development and psychopathology. Beginning with Freud, there has always been greater focus on the intrapsychic rather than the interpersonal. Indeed, there has often been a purposeful exclusion of families, seeing them as detrimental to the individual. And certainly our current psychiatric diagnostic paradigm demands an individual perspective.

Given its demonstrated effectiveness (particularly with children and adolescents) and our ethical obligation to provide clients with the most effective available treatment approaches, it is critical that counselors overcome their reluctance to work with families and begin to include families in treatment—whether it be family therapy only or in combination with other treatments. Therapists can overcome their hesitancy to work with families by reading more about family treatment approaches, attending seminars, seeking supervision/consultation and taking professional risks.

Counselor Cautions

When working with families, if for any reason a counselor suspects that a child has been or is being abused or neglected, s/he must report this to the appropriate child protection agency. Counselors should have their local phone number for reporting abuse or neglect in an easily accessible place.

While joining with a family is extremely important, care should be taken to avoid over-identification with a single family member. By the same token, care should also be taken to avoid feelings of disapproval towards a single family member. Families are sensitive to the possibility of a therapist favoring (or disfavoring) individual family members. Counselors should be alert to the possibility of various types of countertransference and should always be attentive to therapist–client boundaries.

Purpose of this Book

The purpose of this book is to educate therapists about several at-risk family types and to provide specific activities to address the family functioning needs of these families. It will describe some of the vulnerabilities and strengths of the various types of families and will describe the type(s) of family intervention(s) that may be needed. Specific and engaging discussion questions are included, along with games, activities and rituals for each type of family. In providing this information, the authors hope to reduce counselor anxiety regarding working with family systems.

References

Carr, A. (2009a) "The effectiveness of family therapy and systemic interventions for child-focused problems." *Journal of Family Therapy 31*, 3–45.

Carr, A. (2009b) "The effectiveness of family therapy and systemic interventions for adult-focused problems." *Journal of Family Therapy 31*, 46–74.

Miller, W. and Rollnick, S. (2002) *Motivational Interviewing: Preparing People for Change* (2nd edition). New York: Guildford Press.

Minuchin, S. (1974) *Families and Family Therapy*. London: Tavistock.

Robbins, M.S., Turner, C.W., Alexander, J.F. and Perez, G.A. (2003) "Alliance and dropout in family therapy for adolescents with behavior problems: individual and systemic effects." *Journal of Family Psychology 17*, 4, 534–544.

Shadish, W. and Baldwin, S. (2003) "Meta-analysis of MFT interventions." *Journal of Marital and Family Therapy 29*, 547–570.

Worden, M. (2002) *Family Therapy Basics*. Independence, KY: Cengage Learning.

CHAPTER 2
Family Assessment

Purpose of Assessment

Family assessment identifies, explores and ponders both a family's problems and their strengths. It seeks to understand the structure, the functioning and the influences that affect a family and contributes to their identified problem(s). Similar to assessments with individuals, family assessment is critical to informing treatment decisions. According to McPhatter (1991) a family assessment should include the following areas.

- A clear description of the problem including its history, its intensity over time, various family members' interpretations, past solutions, intergenerational patterns and family members' motivation in treatment.

- An account of the family's organization including membership, power, socioeconomic status and cultural influences.

- Details about family functioning including lifecycle issues, roles, rules, communication style and problem-resolution skills.

- Family strengths and resources.

There are many ways to assess families—such as interviews, ecomaps, genograms, family sculptures, observations and self-report questionnaires. Selecting the appropriate family assessment technique(s) requires some reflection. When deciding on assessment tools, it is important to consider the following points.

1. What areas of family functioning need to be assessed?

2. Does the assessment technique(s) match the family members' developmental stage?

3. Does the assessment "fit" the family's traits?

4. Will the assessment technique only be used to form a treatment plan or will it also be used to monitor progress on an ongoing basis?

5. Is the assessment technique culturally sensitive?

6. Is the instrument evidence based? Is there psychometric data available?

When assessing families, counselors should pay special attention to the family's strengths as well as their complaints. All families have qualities that suggest resiliency and healthy functioning. According to Schene (2005) and Gladding (2007) these qualities can include:

- the presence of a supportive extended family and community
- the valuing of and commitment to the family unit and its members
- the ability of family members to control anger expression
- the physical and emotional health of the parent(s) or caregiver(s)
- the understanding of parent(s) or caregiver(s) of children's developmental needs
- the ability to adapt to change, including the changing needs of family members
- the ability of family members to accept responsibility for their own behavior
- the ability to set appropriate boundaries
- effective communication including problem-solving
- appreciation and affection for one another.

Interviews

A thorough interview is the most basic but also the most essential assessment technique. A comprehensive interview is fundamental in obtaining a better understanding of a family's history and perception of the problem. Good interview skills include asking relevant questions, seeking clarification, listening attentively, observing nonverbal messages and identifying important feelings, thoughts and interactions. Typically, open-ended questions rather than closed-ended questions allow family members to talk more freely and to address the issues that they think are important. In order to keep an interview from sounding like an interrogation, however, it is also important for the counselor to empathically reflect what s/he believes s/he has heard from the family. Mirroring both the verbal and nonverbal messages is part of reflective listening and accurate empathy.

In addition to basic informational questions, circular questions can assist the counselor by focusing on family connections/distinctions and avoiding the trap of only working on one particular family member's symptomology. Circular questions not only assist the therapist in obtaining important information, they also provide the family with new information about themselves. Palazzoli *et al.* (1978) suggest beginning circular questioning with the youngest family members. Examples of circular questions are listed here.

- Who in the family is most concerned about this problem? If the problem sticks around for several more years, who will be the most concerned then?
- Which two members of this family get along the best?
- Which two members of this family have the most conflict?

13

- Who spends the most time together?

- Who has the most *influence on feelings* in this family? Who can make people feel a certain way faster than anyone else? How does s/he do it?

- Who is the family comedian or *family clown*? In other words, who is in charge of keeping things light (less uptight) in this family?

- On a scale of one to ten, how stubborn is each family member?

- How is your family like and different from other families?

- How do long periods of feeling angry/anxious/depressed etc. affect family relationships?

- *<To children only>* What causes your parent(s) the most stress, worry, and sadness? What brings them the most satisfaction, pleasure, and peace?

- *<To children only>* What makes your parent(s) proudest about you? What do they worry about for you?

Interviews can be helpful in family assessments to:

- engage the family in treatment

- identify the family's priorities regarding the problem

- obtain clarification of family members' perceptions

- expand on the existing information.

Genograms

A genogram is a diagram of multiple family generations that goes beyond a simple family tree. It identifies repetitive intergenerational patterns of behavior that may influence the current nuclear family (McGoldrick and Gerson 1985). It also enables the family to step back a bit, examine themselves in a broader context and gain insight into complex family dynamics that have developed over time.

Important and relevant information can often be obtained through a genogram. Some of the data that is recorded on a genogram can include education, occupations, illnesses, emotional relationships, alcoholism, depression, family alliances and family conflicts. Other family dynamics that may emerge through the use of the genogram are emotional cut-offs, triangulations and family differentiation.

There are variations on how to diagram certain family situations and relationships, but basic symbols include: squares for males; circles for women; single, horizontal lines for marriage; one slanted line through the horizontal line for separation; and two slanted lines through the horizontal line for divorce. Typically the oldest child is below and to the left of her/his parents, whereas the youngest is below and to the right.

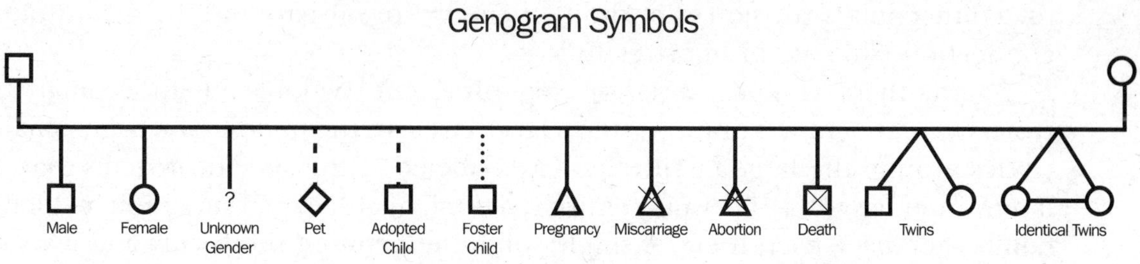

Genogram Symbols

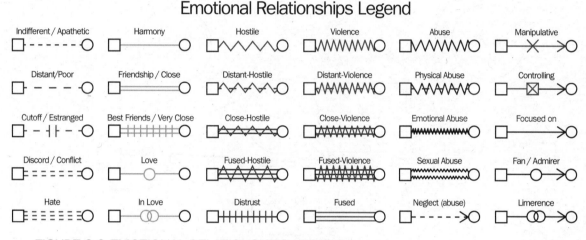

FIGURE 2.1 GENOGRAM SYMBOLS

Emotional relationships also have symbols that help describe family dynamics.

Emotional Relationships Legend

FIGURE 2.2 EMOTIONAL RELATIONSHIPS LEGEND

Genograms can be helpful in family assessments to:

- find intergenerational patterns that might be contributing to the problem
- gain insight about the "presence of the past" in the here and now
- reduce guilt and blame by setting the problem in a larger context
- understand the roots of family worldviews and values.

Ecomaps

An ecomap is a diagram that maps a family's relationships with its community systems—a map of the family system in its environment. Its focus is on the ecological system in which the family is embedded (Hartman 1995). It may be helpful to think of an ecomap as a "solar system" where the family is placed in the center (i.e. the "sun") and other important people and institutions are placed in circles around the center (i.e. the "planets"). Lines between the family and each person/ institution show the strength of the connection (weak or strong), the impact of the connection (provision of or drain of energy/resources) and the quality of the connection (stressful or not stressful).

Again, there is some variation regarding the symbols in an ecomap but typically a genogram is drawn inside a large circle in the middle of a page. Smaller circles around the large family circle are labeled as the specific systems that the family interacts with—i.e. work, church, school, health care, recreation, extended family members, friends etc. A single solid line between the family and a system represents a strong connection; three solid lines indicates an intense relationship; a broken line indicates a tenuous relationship; and a zigzag line shows a stressful/conflictual relationship. Arrows can also be drawn on the connection lines to indicate the direction of the flow of resources and energy.

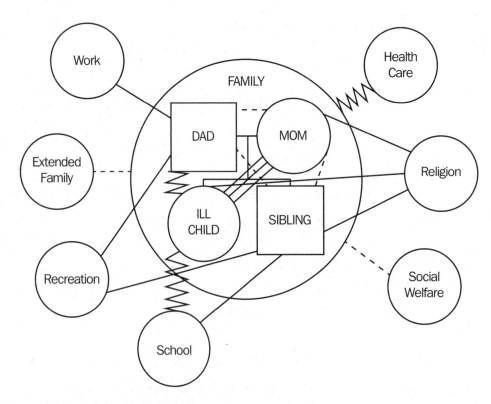

FIGURE 2.3 AN ECOMAP

Ecomaps can be helpful in family assessments to:

- gain a larger perspective regarding a family's ecosystem
- identify external resources or lack thereof
- recognize the permeability of a family's boundary
- identify stressors and points of conflict that need to be mediated.

Kinetic Family Drawing

A kinetic family drawing is a projective art assessment. It asks individual family members to draw a picture of her/his entire family "doing something" (i.e. some kind of action) (Burns and Kaufman 1970). Traditionally used with children, all family members may do their own drawings although there is some controversy regarding the validity of adult drawings. Pictures are meant to elicit attitudes about the family and overall family dynamics by bypassing defenses and family censors (Klorer 2006).

Pictures are examined for action, style and symbols. *Action* refers to the movement of energy between people. Action between family members may show high energy, such as some kind of competitive play, or it may show low energy, such as two people sitting or looking away from one another. *Style* refers to the method with which the picture is drawn. This would include an examination of the picture for barriers and lines in addition to individual characteristics of family members and their positions. *Symbols* refer to the inclusion of items such as balls, snakes, flowers, etc. However, interpretation of symbols should be done with caution, as there may be multiple interpretations for a single symbol.

It is suggested that, when using the kinetic family drawing, the counselor ask questions in order to obtain additional information. In particular, it may be helpful to ask what the figures are doing, feeling and thinking. It is also suggested that counselors observe the family member's behavior (reactions and verbalizations) while drawing.

Kinetic family drawings can be helpful in family assessments to:

- bypass defenses and access the unconscious or unspoken aspects of family life

- engage shy, nonverbal family members

- recognize individual family members' perceptions of the family

- understand boundaries, roles and power within the family.

Family Sculptures

A family sculpture is a psychodrama technique that asks individual family members to take turns physically placing other family members in positions that show their relation to one another. Family members act as "sculptors" and use closeness/distance, body posture and props to demonstrate their perception of each family member's relationship to the others—an "in vivo" arrangement of people (Duhl, Kantor and Duhl 1973). As such, the space between people and their physical postures becomes a physical description about relationships.

Some counselors have used the sculpting method to explore family perceptions over time. Instead of simply asking family members to position one another as they currently perceive their relationships, they are also asked to create sculptures of the family at a moment in time in the past and/or how they imagine family relationships to be in the future.

Family sculptures can be helpful in family assessments to:

- clarify family roles
- understand the family's cohesion and closeness/distance factors
- identify alignments and triangulation patterns
- identify communication patterns.

Observations

Most of our communicated information is not sent through words. It is sent through nonverbal expressions. People often try to hide feelings behind carefully chosen words, but gestures, facial expressions, voice tone, use of space and timing are more honest conveyers of feelings and attitudes. With that said, however, there is no dictionary of nonverbal communication. Basic facial expressions are dependent on culture, context and individual differences, so it is important for counselors to interpret behavior with care. However, some questions counselors may consider as they observe family interactions are listed here.

- Who attends the sessions regularly and who misses sessions regularly?
- How are family members arranged in the room? Who sits next to whom?
- Do parents look at one another when the other speaks? What are their facial expressions?
- Do family members hear each other out or do they interrupt one another? Who tends to do the most interrupting? Who tends to get interrupted?
- Who does the most speaking? Who gets spoken to the most? Who gets ignored?
- What is the tone of the communication between family members? Is it conflictual, aggressive, critical, sarcastic, sincere, objective or super rational?
- Do family members appear to understand one another's meanings?
- Are there positive touches, head nods and smiles exchanged between family members?
- Who shifts in their chairs when certain topics are raised?

Not only does a counselor make observations during an interview, s/he might also give the family a specific assignment or enactment and then observe the members' interactions as they complete the task. For example, the counselor may ask the family to draw a mural together or to plan a trip together. The counselor then observes how family members cooperate and communicate with each other, how they make decisions, what roles individual members play and what problems arise etc.

Observations can be helpful in family assessments to:

- identify communication patterns and power structures
- recognize alignments and triangulations
- discover levels of affection and warmth
- identify topics of discomfort and conflict.

Self-Report Questionnaires

Self-report questionnaires are pencil-and-paper forms, which family members complete. They provide a measurable means to determine individual family members' perceptions, feelings and behaviors. There are very many self-report measures available, which provide information on a wide variety of family dimensions. Some are comprehensive and measure several family domains while others measure only one very specific domain. Examples of these domains include family stress, cohesion, adaptability, problem-solving, roles, affective responsiveness, conflict, communication, parenting practices and parenting stress. Some of the better known self-report instruments include the Family Adaptability and Cohesion Evaluation Scale (FACES IV), the McMaster Family Assessment Device (FAD), the Family Environment Scale (FES) and the Self-Report Family Inventory (SFI), the Conflict Tactics Scale (CTS) and the Parenting Stress Index (PSI).

A self-report instrument should show evidence of validity and reliability. Counselors should also have knowledge regarding the concepts that are being measured and possess adequate understanding of different populations in order to place results in a cultural context.

Self-report questionnaires can be helpful in family assessments to:

- compare scores with normative samples regarding specific problems

- measure the intensity of a problem

- allow members a safe medium for disclosing information that might not be revealed in an interview

- measure outcomes through the use of pre- and post-tests.

References

Burns, R.C. and Kaufman, S.H. (1970) *Kinetic Family Drawings: An Introduction to Understanding Children Through Kinetic Drawings.* New York: Brunner/Mazel.

Duhl, F., Kantor, D. and Duhl, B. (1973) "Learning Space and Action in Family Therapy." In D. Block (ed.) *Techniques of Family Psychotherapy: A Primer.* New York: Grune and Stratton.

Gladding, S.T. (2007) *Family Therapy: History, Theory, and Practice* (5th edition). Upper Saddle River, NJ: Prentice Hall.

Hartman, A. (1995) "Diagrammatic assessment of family relationships." *Families in Society 76,* 111–122.

Klorer, P.G. (2006) "Art Therapy with Traumatized Families." In L. Carey (ed.) *Expressive and Creative Arts Methods for Trauma Survivors.* London: Jessica Kingsley Publishers.

McGoldrick, M. and Gerson, R. (1985) *Genograms in Family Assessment.* New York: Norton.

McPhatter, A.R. (1991) "Assessment revisited: a comprehensive approach to understanding family dynamics." *Families in Society 72,* 11–21.

Palazzoli, S.M., Boscolo, L., Cecchin, G. and Prata, G. (1978) *Paradox and Counterparadox: A New Model in the Therapy of the Family in Schizophrenic Transaction.* New York: Jason Aronson.

Schene, P. (2005) *Comprehensive Family Assessment Guidelines for Child Welfare.* New York: National Resource Center for Family-Centered Practice and Permanency Planning, A Service of the Children's Bureau.

CHAPTER 3

Single-Parent Families with an Absent Parent

Introduction

Research in the United States has seen an increase in the number of families headed by a single parent. In 2000 alone, single-parent families headed by mothers increased to ten million from three million in 1970 and households headed by fathers increased from 393,000 to over two million in the same timeframe (Hornberger, Zabriskie and Freeman 2010). One usually thinks of single-parent families as headed by mothers; however there has also been a great increase in homes headed by single fathers. For the purposes of this chapter, the definition of single-parent families is families where there is not another parent available. While numbers regarding mother-absent families are unavailable, Kelly and Emery (2003) report that 20 percent of children are estranged or abandoned by a father as a result of parental divorce.

As the prevalence of single-parent families increases, the variations of the types of single-parent families have increased as well. Some single parents live in poverty; others are financially stable. Some live alone with their children; others live with parents, friends or other family members. Some have the financial support and involvement of the other parent; others have none. Some have always been single or have chosen to be single parents through adoption or artificial insemination; others were previously married or are widowed. Some have an extensive network of supportive family and friends; others have no one that they can identify as a support.

Potential Challenges/Vulnerabilities

Challenges for single-parent households often include economic vulnerability, isolation, feelings of guilt and parentification of the children in the home. It is likely that the basic tasks of everyday survival—performing chores or responsibilities— will take a great proportion of the single parent's energy, creating less time to appropriately take care of him/herself. Single parents must manage their children, a household and a job, and hopefully be able to have a social life, without going under and without the assistance of a partner to help with any type of emergency.

Compared with their married counterparts, single parents work longer hours, face more stressful life changes, are more frequently depressed and have more economic problems and less emotional support in performing their parent role (Anderson 2003). For single parents who are isolated, their difficulty in functioning as a single parent is increased. Without the support of others, including but not limited to family members, friends, church, schools etc., single parents can find it difficult to complete everyday activities without extreme stress. Single parents without support have greater financial and childcare strains.

Financial hardship is frequently noted to be the most significant challenge to being a single parent. Often, these low-income single parents live completely on the edge of crisis, meaning that they are acutely aware that some emergency need for increased funds or some break in their routine can push them over the edge into chaos (Anderson 2003). Single-parent families are more than twice as likely to have stressful family environments as their dual-parent counterparts (Moore and Vandivere 2000) and therefore less time to devote towards leisure activities that can aid in building and supporting family cohesion.

Single parents generally experience feelings of being spread thin, leading them to use their children as sources of support. It is common to hear a parent boast about their son becoming, "the man of the house," or their daughter taking on household duties such as meal preparation or housework. Children learning responsibility and taking part in participation in household chores should be a part of any household, however it is when children obtain a sense of "my mom/dad needs me," that issues can arise. This can cause problems with boundaries and result in a parentified child. Parentified children are generally less likely to get along with their peers, as they are often considered bossy and may challenge other authority figures in their roles because they have been taught to make decisions that are outside of their developmental range (Rober 2010).

Research suggests that adolescents from single-parent households are more prone to delinquent behaviors, teen pregnancy, social problems, lower academic achievement and high school dropout (Dunifon and Kowaleski-Jones 2002; Hemovich and Crano 2009; McLanahan and Sandefur 1994). There is some indication that behavioral problems may be more problematic for boys than for girls in single-parent families (Griffin *et al.* 2000). It also appears that children living with widowed mothers have fewer behavioral problems than those being raised by other kinds of single mothers (McLanahan and Sandefur 1994). While there may be several explanations for this, an important one is the fact that widowed mothers may have additional resources and support. Children in father-only households reported substantially more drug use than children in either mother-only or dual-parent households. This was more problematic for girls living with their fathers than boys living with their fathers (Hemovick and Crano 2009).

Although the prevalence of single-parent families has increased, the stigma they experience seems to remain present. Single parents harbor guilt over the effects that they feel they are having on their child/children. Single parents may feel guilty for several different reasons including:

- financial constraints—inability to provide requested material items, decreased leisure activities, "We can't have Christmas like we used to," "You can only play one sport"

- reduced time together

- feeling the need to replace the absent parent or fulfill the role of the absent parent

- allowing the child to engage in inappropriate behavior.

Strengths

All single-parent families have strengths that can assist them in solving problems and functioning as a healthy household. There is a stigma that single-parent families are impoverished women living on welfare with two or more children. However, single parenthood is growing across all socioeconomic groups.

Single-parent families often use adversity to strengthen their family through efforts to create communal coping, improve relationships and new family rituals, which create a sense of belonging and identifying as a family (Hutchinson, Afifi and Krause 2007). The choice to become a single parent can also be one made in order to keep that parent and/or child safe due to a dangerous situation or unhealthy relationship.

Empirical Support for Treatment

Family functioning is a delicate combination between family cohesion and family adaptability (Olson 1993). Although single-parent families face challenges, it cannot be assumed that they will not succeed. Many families adapt well to a single-parent household and are as healthy and well functioning as any other household. Increased parental monitoring and eating family dinners together ameliorates children's externalizing behaviors such as social problems and lower academic achievement (Griffin *et al.* 2000).

Larson, Dworkin and Gillman (2001) examined the characteristics of well-functioning mother-only families to identify behaviors related to positive adaptation to the demands of single-parent family life. It was concluded that many families adjust positively to single parenthood. The following family management variables were types of parent behaviors most related to decreasing behavioral issues.

- Firm discipline or structure.

- Consistent meaningful family routines.

- Parent's time spent on child-supportive activities.

Family leisure involvement has been identified as an essential part of health family functioning (Zabriskie and Freeman 2004). Although single parents may not be able to participate in as many leisure activities due to less time, effort or money being available, limited participation is better than none. There are two different types of family leisure activities—core and balance.

- Core family leisure activities include family involvement in activities that are typically home based, common and accessible, and are ordinary activities that family members engage in often. These activities are more likely to be utilized in single-parent homes as they are in an "at-home" setting, such as playing games inside or out, cooking or eating dinner together. Hutchinson *et al.* (2007) found that participation in core activities in single-parent families were very important to help family members stay connected, feel a sense of belonging and demonstrate care for each other.

- Balance leisure activities are less regular, are out of the ordinary and are done less often, making them more unique. Examples include traveling, vacations, participating in outdoor activities away from home, such as camping or fishing. These activities generally take more time, effort and money than core activities.

Resources

- Single Parent Advocate—tips for parenting and accessing resources: www.singleparentadvocate.org

- Single Parents Network—information and resources for single parents http://singleparentsnetwork.com

- National Mentoring Partnership: www.mentoring.org/about_mentor/value_of_mentoring

- Explaining an Absent Parent to Young Children: www.onefamily.ie/wp-content/uploads/Level-4-Relationships-Explaining-an-Absent-Parent.pdf

- How Do You Deal with an Absent Parent: www.singlemommyhood.com/2009/05/how-do-deal-with-an-absent-parent

Counselor Cautions

Boundaries are important in every therapeutic relationship, however single parents can easily invite therapists to fill in the gap left by the absent parent. A parent may invite the therapist to act in a strict father-like way, while another parent may present with such sadness, as to evoke consoling actions from the therapist (Rober 2010). While empathy is what therapy provides, it is important to continuously monitor the parent's response to your consoling actions in order to not be misconstrued as an emotional replacement for the absent parent. As with any therapeutic relationship, it is especially important to avoid social isolation of the family and to try to reconnect the family to its social support system.

While engagement with all families is important, it is particularly critical with single-parent families, as they have been shown to drop out of treatment prematurely (McKay and Bannon 2004). Counselors should make extra efforts to help single parents feel accepted in treatment and should take extra time to address any barriers to treatment.

Discussion Questions

- What are your family's strengths?

- What would it be like if you had more frequent meals together? If that is something that you like, how could you make that happen?

- What types of activities would make time together more fun?

- What are the obstacles to having more fun together? How could you overcome these?

- What friends or extended family members can all of you count on?

- Who makes the rules in your family? Who do you think *should* make rules for your family?

- Does <*single parent*> take care of her/himself? Do you ever worry about her/him?

- Utilizing the genogram from Chapter 2—discuss the themes (problems and strengths) of other single-parent families. Examine the extended family in the genogram by asking, "Looking at the other single-parent families in your genogram what strengths/vulnerabilities do you see or have?"

Ideas for Between-Session Homework

- Make time for leisure activities. These can be activities that cost little to no money. They can include picnics, board game nights, swimming, cheap movies, taking a loaf of old bread to a duck pond, bike rides, walks, etc.

- Arrange to have family dinner at least one night a week—the more often the better. The family should sit down at the table together for dinner and then play "High/Low"—where each family member gives a high point of their day and a low point of their day.

- If there is an issue that needs to be discussed with the family hold a family meeting. This can be fun and creative. Make sure that it allows the opportunity for each family member to provide input to the current issue at hand.

- Create a chore chart to make the household duties easier to handle. Make sure to delegate age-appropriate chores and allow all members to have input in the creation of the chart.

- At least once a month the single parent should have a "night out." Arrange to have another family member or friend keep your child/children in order to be able to have a night to yourself. There's one rule: no housework! Use this time to pamper yourself. This does not necessarily need to cost money. It can be catching up on your favorite book, taking a bubble bath, going to dinner with a friend, going to a movie etc.

Therapeutic Activities

Activities included in this section are variations of evidenced-based practices tailored to be utilized with single-parent families. Not all activities will apply to every family. Counselors should select those activities that best address a specific family's problem(s).

MOTHER, MAY I?

PARTICIPANTS
Parent/caregiver and children (ages 3–7)

PURPOSE
To support rules and parent–child boundaries and to increase impulse control

MATERIALS

- None

DESCRIPTION
Explain to the family that it can be easy at times for roles in the family to blur, especially when the parent/caregiver sometimes has to rely on the child/ren to take on extra responsibilities. Discuss the importance of maintaining solid parent–child boundaries. In the traditional game of Mother, May I? the parent/caregiver will play the role of the "Mother"* and the "Child" will be played by any others participating in the session and can be played by anyone.

    * The "Mother" can also be played by other adult family members/family friends present for the session, but do *not* allow the child to be the "Mother."

    Have the child/ren stand about ten feet away from the Mother. The Mother will then give instructions to the child (for example, "Take two steps forward."). Before following the instructions the Child should ask, "Mother, may I?" Mother then responds, "Yes, you may," or "No, you may not," and then the child follows the instructions. Repeat until the child makes it across the room. As the game continues, Mother will continue to give instructions. If the child follows an instruction before stating, "Mother, may I?" they are sent back to the starting point.

DISCUSSION QUESTIONS

- How successful were you in playing this game? Why do you think this was?

- What made the game difficult or frustrating?

- Why is it important for the parent to be the leader for the family?

- Why are rules needed in a family?

- Who is the best one in your family to make the rules?

- This game also teaches impulse control—how do you think it does that?

PAPER STACK

PARTICIPANTS

Parent/caregiver and children (ages 5–6 and up)

PURPOSE

To build family cohesion and problem-solving

MATERIALS

- Ten sheets of paper per family member*

*Any size of paper will work; recycled paper is perfect

DESCRIPTION

Explain to the family that family cohesion is essentially the family's ability to work well together. In order to work well together, we must be able to effectively problem-solve. Give each family member ten sheets of paper and instruct them to build a single tower *together.* They are to build the tower as high as they can *only* using the sheets of paper. (Note: the trick is to fold and balance the sheets of paper—but let the family figure this out on their own.)

DISCUSSION QUESTIONS

- What was it like thinking about tackling this task before you actually began? Did you think you could do it?

- What was it like to work with your family members on this project? What were the contributions of the individual members?

- Did you ever feel discouraged as you were building together?

- What made the task easier? What made it harder?

- What helped you to be successful?

- What did you learn about working together with your family?

IT TAKES A VILLAGE

PARTICIPANTS
Parent/caregiver and children (ages 6–18)

PURPOSE
To identify family supports and assist family members in accessing these supports

MATERIALS
- Cardboard building blocks
- Paper*
- Drawing utensils
- Picture of the family (prior to the session, ask the family to bring with them a family picture) or game pieces representing each family member (if the family was unable to bring their picture)
- Tape

*Any size of paper will work; recycled paper is perfect

DESCRIPTION
Share with the family how important supports are to all families. Explain that in this activity they will be identifying all of their support systems. Then instruct the family to select one person to be the "scribe." Tell the other family members to brainstorm all of the various supportive people, agencies and groups they can think of and have the "scribe" write these down one at a time on single sheets of paper. After the "scribe" has written these down direct the family to wrap the sheets around the blocks, using tape to secure the sheets (one sheet per block) and to stack them. Then ask the family to place their family picture or the game pieces representing their family on top of the blocks, giving the image of the support systems holding them up.

DISCUSSION QUESTIONS
- How does it feel to be on the top with all the support beneath you?
- What makes each one of these blocks a good support?
- Who is the easiest support to access? Who is the hardest?
- What are the steps that you would have to take in order to engage each of these supports?

FAMILY SHIELD

PARTICIPANTS

Parent/caregiver and children (ages 4–18)

PURPOSE

To increase cooperation, build cohesion and identify strengths of the family

MATERIALS

- Paper*
- Drawing utensils

*Any size of paper will work; recycled paper is perfect

DESCRIPTION

Explain to the family the importance of identifying their family's strengths. Share that sometimes we have strengths that we do not even realize are there and that it is through our strengths that we find ways to handle difficult situations. Encourage the family to really think about their strengths. Then instruct the family to work together to create a family crest to signify their family's values and importance to one another.

DISCUSSION QUESTIONS

- What does each of the items on your crest stand for?
- How does this make your family strong?
- What strengths do you have individually that contribute to your family?
- What did you learn about working together with your family?

PAPER BALL WAR

PARTICIPANTS

Parent/caregiver and children (ages 4–18)

PURPOSE

To participate in a cooperative activity as a family, building cohesion

MATERIALS

- Paper*
- Family Shield (made in a previous session) or another item that can be used as a shield

*Any size of paper will work; recycled paper is perfect

DESCRIPTION

Explain that being a member of a family is similar to being part of a team. Discuss examples of how a "team" is less successful if they do not work together and that there are times when it is necessary for a family to work together as a team. Provide the family with a stack of paper and instruct family members to crumple the pieces of paper up into balls. Do the same for yourself. Have the family place their paper balls in front of them on the floor while you place your paper balls in front of you. Explain that the paper balls are the "ammunition" for a Paper Ball War, Child versus Therapist. If there is more than one child, ask the family to select which child will be the therapist's target. The family will then use their family shield (made in a previous session) or another item for a shield (clipboards/binders) to protect the targeted child from the therapist's paper balls. (The therapist can use a clipboard or binder for her/his shield.) As the Paper Ball War ensues (family throwing at the therapist and therapist throwing at the targeted child), instruct the parent to make protective statements such as, "You can't hurt someone from our family!"

DISCUSSION QUESTIONS

- How did it feel to work together as a family?
- Who are the "protectors" in your family?
- Can you allow your parent to protect you in other ways? How?
- What did you learn about working together with your family?

GUILT GOBBLERS

PARTICIPANTS

Parent/caregiver only

PURPOSE

To decrease parental guilt

MATERIALS

- Paper* or index cards

*Any size of paper will work; recycled paper is perfect

DESCRIPTION

Discuss with the parent/caregiver how guilt is a common feeling associated with being a single parent. Explain that guilt can come in many forms and that often the guilt stems from a situation that is out of the parent/caregiver's control. Provide the parent/caregiver with a set of index cards or several pieces of paper. Instruct them to list separately on each card/piece of paper all the things that make her/him feel as if they are a bad parent. Then sort the cards into two piles of what can be controlled and what cannot. On the cards that can be controlled, the parent should write three solutions on the back. On the cards that cannot be controlled, the parent should tear them up and throw them in the trash or rubbish.

DISCUSSION QUESTIONS

- What does the following phrase mean to you? "Grant me the serenity to accept the things I cannot change, the courage to change the things I can, and the wisdom to know the difference."
- What are going to be the easiest things to change? What about the hardest?
- How does it feel to "get rid" of the guilt?
- What can you do in the future to help recognize the things you can/cannot change?

SWEET SENTIMENTS

PARTICIPANTS
Parent/caregiver and children (ages 4–18)

PURPOSE
To increase cooperation, cohesion and the recognition of individual strengths

MATERIALS

- 1 bag of Skittles or other colored sweets

DESCRIPTION
Discuss with the family how it is easier to point out the negative things about a person or a situation than the positive things. Explain that recognizing and identifying strengths increases self-esteem and improves mood, which in turn makes it easier to be around each other. Discuss that sometimes one person's negativity can affect the whole family. Divide the bag of Skittles among each family member, making sure that each person has the same amount of sweets. Instruct each family member to sort their pile by color. As they sort, they should do the following thing for each color.

- Green—say something about yourself that you like.
- Yellow—say something about someone else in the family that you like.
- Purple—say things you would like to do together as a family.
- Orange—say rules that you think are good ones.
- Red—say what you could do more of to make your family better.

DISCUSSION QUESTIONS

- How did it feel to have someone say nice things about you?

- How did it feel to say nice things about others in your family?

- Did any of the compliments surprise you? Why?

- What are the rules that you did not choose? Are there things that can make those rules better?

- Did you learn anything about another family member that you didn't know?

- How can being more positive help your family?

- What things can you do to help yourself to remember to be more positive?

- What are ways to remind your family members to be more positive without making them feel bad?

BOUNDARY PIES

PARTICIPANTS
Parent/caregiver and children (ages 12–18)

PURPOSE
Building and understanding boundaries between parents and adolescents

MATERIALS

- Paper* with pie charts and ages listed underneath them (see example below)

- Two different colors of crayons/markers

*Any size of paper will work; recycled paper is perfect

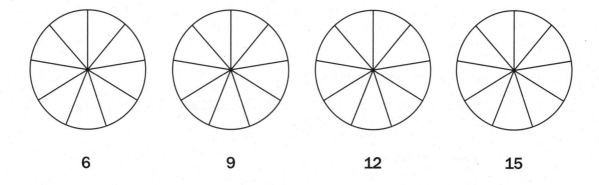

| 6 | 9 | 12 | 15 |

DESCRIPTION
Share with the family members that when relying on each other a great deal is essential and that boundaries can become blurred. As children get older they are given more responsibilities and freedoms, but we have to remember that there must still be rules and respect for one another. Give each person a sheet of paper with the Boundary Pies drawn on them. Explain that the pies represent rules and the numbers represent

different ages. For each pie, family members should color in (any color can be used) sections to represent what proportion of the rules people of that age should follow *without negotiation* between the parent/caregiver and the child/ren. They should color the remaining sections in a different color to show what proportion of the rules *can* be negotiated. Once complete, adolescents should pick the pie that they are closest to in age and discuss.

DISCUSSION QUESTIONS

- How do you respond to the rules in your home?

- Do you try to negotiate rules now? If so, look at the pie that is closest to your age. How is what you colored in similar or different to how you actually respond to rules at home?

- How are your proportions different from your parent's?

- Which rules are non-negotiable? Which ones can be negotiated? Why?

- How does it feel to be able to give your input into rules as you get older?

- Was there a particular age where what you colored in was very different from your parent's? Was there a particular age where it was close to being the same?

SINGLE-PARENT FAMILY BOARD GAME

PARTICIPANTS
Parent/caregiver and children (age 5 and up)

PURPOSE
To enhance communication and cohesion

MATERIALS

- Snakes and Ladders board game

- Appendix A cards (discussion, feelings and interactions)

- Appendix B cards (single parent)

- Colored copy paper

- Scissors

DESCRIPTION
Prior to the family's arrival, make photocopies of the four sets of game cards using four different colors of copy paper (or simply write "Single Parent," "Discussion," "Interactions" and "Feelings" on the backs of the appropriate cards). Cut these out and place the game cards into four piles on the table. Then play Snakes and Ladders (moving up or down the board if you land on a ladder or a snake) with a difference—when players land on a numbered space they must answer a question from one of the

four sets of cards. If they land on numbers 1–25 they should answer a "Feelings" card; if they land on numbers 26–50 they should answer an "Interactions" card; if they land on numbers 51–75 they should answer a "Single Parent" card; if they land on numbers 76–100 they should answer a "Discussion" card. The first player to reach the top wins.

DISCUSSION QUESTIONS

- What was it like playing a game with your family?
- Were you surprised by anyone's answers to the game cards? Whose and why?
- What did you learn about yourself and your family members from this game?
- Were there any thoughts, feelings or ideas you wanted to express during the game but didn't get to? What were they?
- What additional questions do you have for your family after playing this game?
- Did anything in the game inspire you to want to change something in yourself or in your family?

NO RULES GAME

PARTICIPANTS
Parent/caregiver and children (ages 4 and up)

PURPOSE
To support rules and boundaries

MATERIALS

- Deck of cards

DESCRIPTION
Explain to family members that there are rules everywhere. While some rules may seem unfair or ridiculous, they are usually in place for a reason. Give the deck of cards to the children in the family. Direct them to play a game with the cards that none of them have ever played before. Tell them that there can be no rules.

DISCUSSION QUESTIONS

- How successful were you in playing a game? Why was this?
- What made the game difficult or frustrating?
- Why are rules needed in a game?
- Why are rules needed in a family?
- Who is the best one in your family to make the rules?

Additional Activities That May be Helpful

- "Peace" of the Pie in Chapter 6: Families with Grandparents as Caregivers (p.80)

- Family Traditions in Chapter 7: Families with an Incarcerated Loved One (p.94)

- Reflecting, Reflecting, Reflecting in Chapter 7: Families with an Incarcerated Loved One (p.96)

- Sizing up Supervision Chapter 8: Families with a Substance Abusing Child (p.115)

- Parenting Consistency in Chapter 9: Families with Parent Substance Abuse (p.129)

- My Worry Box in Chapter 10: Families with a Mentally Ill Parent (p.146)

- A Bag of Coping in Chapter 10: Families with a Mentally Ill Parent (p.148)

References

Anderson, C. (2003) "The Diversity, Strengths, and Challenges of Single Parent Households." In F. Walsh (ed.) *Normal Family Processes: Growing Diversity and Complexity* (3rd edition). New York: Guilford Press.

Dunifon, R. and Kowaleski-Jones, L. (2002) "Who's in the house? Race differences in cohabitation, single parenthood and child development." *Child Development 73*, 4, 1249–2664.

Griffin, K.W., Botvin, G.J., Scheier, L.M., Diaz, T. and Miller, N.L. (2000) "Parenting practices as predictors of substance use, delinquency, and aggression among urban minority youth: moderating effects of family structure and gender." *Psychology of Addictive Behaviors 14*, 2, 174–184.

Hemovich, V. and Crano, W.D. (2009) "Family structure and adolescent drug use: an exploration of single-parent families." *Substance Use and Misuse 44*, 14, 2099–2113.

Hornberger, B., Zabriskie, R.B. and Freeman, P. (2010) "Contributions of family leisure to family functioning among single-parent families." *Leisure Sciences 32*, 143–161.

Hutchinson, S., Afifi, T. and Krause, S. (2007) "The family that plays together fares better: examining the contribution of shared family time to family resilience following divorce." *Journal of Divorce and Remarriage 46*, 3/4, 21–48.

Kelly, J.B. and Emery, R.E. (2003) "Children's adjustment following divorce: risk and resiliency perspectives." *Family Relations 52*, 352–362.

Larson, R., Dworkin, J. and Gillman, S. (2001) "Facilitating adolescents' constructive use of time in one-parent families." *Applied Developmental Science 5*, 3, 143–158.

McKay, M.M. and Bannon, Jr., W.M. (2004) "Engaging families in child mental health services." *Child Adolescent Psychiatric Clinic of North America 13*, 905–921.

McLanahan, S. and Sandefur, G. (1994) *Growing Up with a Single Parent: What Helps, What Hurts.* Cambridge, MA: Harvard University Press.

Moore, K. and Vandivere, S. (2000) *Stressful Family Lives: Child and Parent Well-being.* Washington: Urban Institute. Available at www.urban.org/url.cfm?id=309565, accessed on 2 October 2013.

Olson, D. (1993) "Circumplex Model of Marital and Family Systems: Assessing Family Systems." In F. Walks (ed.) *Normal Family Processes.* New York: Guilford Press.

Rober, P. (2010) "The single-parent family and the family therapist: about invitations and positioning." *The Australian and New Zealand Journal of Family Therapist 31*, 3, 221–231.

Zabriskie, R. and Freeman, P. (2004) "Contributions of family leisure to family functioning among transracial adoptive families." *Adoption Quarterly 7*, 3, 49–77.

CHAPTER 4

Divorced/Separated/Unmarried Families—Both parents available

Introduction

According to the CDC's National Vital Statistics System (2011) approximately 40 percent of marriages end in divorce. Although rates have dropped from 50 percent over the last decade, the rate is still extremely high (Trust 2013). When divorce occurs, it presents an enormous change in family life. For most couples with children, it does not represent the end to their family, but rather the restructuring of their family (Iowa State University 1996). While divorce is defined as the termination of a marital union, for purposes of this chapter the term "divorced" is intended to include those parents who were never legally married but lived as married and are now separated. These families will experience similar emotional impact and restructuring. Restructuring families is stressful, affecting such areas as:

- finances
- parent roles
- household duties
- schedules
- rules.

The impact of divorce is well documented in the literature and addresses the losses that are experienced by both adults and children (Bottom 2013). For adults it includes the grief around the loss of an identity and the family dream, reduced resources and possibly the adjustment to co-parenting while no longer married. For children it is a disruption in their daily lives, adjusting to going back and forth between two households, grief surrounding the loss of the parent they will no longer be residing with full time and financial security.

Women are more likely to initiate divorce than men (Kitson 1992). Divorced men and women state that legal systems are typically more "mother-friendly," especially in terms of child custody (Bottom 2013; Braver and Griffin 2000). Consequently, divorced fathers express more anger toward "the system" (Laasko and Adams 2006).

Potential Challenges/Vulnerabilities

Research has consistently identified that high levels of parental conflict during and after a divorce are associated with poorer child outcomes (e.g. Lebow 2003). These children have higher rates of depression, anxiety and behavior problems, and relationship problems later in life (e.g. Wallerstein and Blakeslee 1996; Heatherington 2002). Adolescents have higher rates of behavioral and emotional problems, as well as drug and alcohol problems (Appell 2006). Obviously, if a couple has ended a committed relationship there will have been conflict present, but the duration, intensity and frequency of the conflict is pertinent to children's adjustment.

Parents with poor communication and poor conflict resolution skills, may make efforts to use children to communicate for them. This places children "in the middle" of parent conflicts. A parent may limit visitation as a way to punish the other parent, thereby depriving the child of needed parental contact. Children can become confused and anxious, and develop resentment towards one parent or place a parent on a pedestal. They may feel torn or under pressure to choose sides.

Parents themselves may have periods of extreme emotional stress, especially if the divorce was due to circumstances out of their control (i.e. initiated by the other party). These parents are at risk of depression, anxiety and substance use, which results in reduced family functioning (Emery 1994). Many divorced individuals report experiencing repeated, intrusive thoughts about their ex-spouses, leading to sadness and confusion at the loss of the relationship (Berman 1988; Weiss 1975). Typically, women experience less stress and better adjustment than men. In fact, Kposowa (2003) reported that divorced men were eight times more likely to commit suicide than were divorced women.

Even in well-adjusting divorced families, struggles may occur regarding effective co-parenting. Despite the severing of the marital relationship, parents must maintain a relationship with one another because of their shared children. It is likely that rules will not be the same at each home and this can create conflict and tension. Other parenting conflicts often surround issues such as religion, school, sports, etc. which can also cause turmoil.

Strengths

Divorce is usually a remedial measure and the decision to separate is intended to improve matters, not make them worse. Marriages end in divorce for many reasons, including partners feeling trapped, incompatibility, abuse, etc. A divorce can provide individuals with an opportunity to "start over."

Although children of divorced parents, as a group, have more adjustment problems than children of never-divorced parents, newer research has documented the negative effects of troubled marriages on children (Kelly 2000). The opportunity to restructure the family can allow for decreased tension and/or conflict and allow for a more favorable environment.

Extended family members often step in to assist with financial and emotional support during this time of restructuring. This additional support can be a very positive influence on children. Increased bonding with grandparents, aunts, uncles, etc. allows children a greater sense of being supported and loved.

Empirical Support for Treatment

Children whose divorced families have strong organization and effective communication function better in a range of areas (Isaacs, Montalvo and Abelsohn 2000). Factors contributing to a child's post-divorce adjustment include parenting style, financial security and the presence/intensity of parent conflict (Gatins, Kinlaw and Dunlap 2013). Appropriate parenting consists of providing emotional support, monitoring children's activities, disciplining authoritatively and maintaining age-appropriate expectations (APA, 2013). Children who have *quality* visits with the non-residential parent, whose parents have low conflict post-divorce and whose parents have joint legal custody are more satisfied and better adjusted (APA 2013).

Isaacs, Montalvo and Abelsohn (2000) found that Divorce Therapy works towards restoring, recovering and reconfiguring family relationships. Its focus is on assisting the reorganization of the family into a functional "two-home family" (Dozier 2004). Principles of Divorce Therapy include:

- focus on more than one affect and perspective
- make sure loss/hurts are acknowledged and addressed
- assist family members in seeing their contributions
- prioritize parental communication
- work for the success of both parents
- strengthen sibling and "new home" subsystems
- reinforce children's obligations to the functioning of the family
- limit influence of antagonistic groups
- control potentially hostile encounters.

Integrative Family Therapy is another therapeutic approach that looks to identify the most prominent factors at work in each family. With these factors a therapeutic plan is developed for the family versus following an invariant method for treating those who present with custody and visitation disputes (Lebow 2003). Interventions include:

- psycho-education—help families to better understand the challenges they are going to face

- creating a solution-oriented focus—the focus of who started the problem is replaced with a focus of how the problem can be solved

- promoting disengagement between parents and a sense of separation between mother's house and father's house—teaching parents to disengage from one another and teaching the child skills to avoid triangulation

- establishing reliable rule-driven methods of communication and "good enough" coordination—creating reliable and agreed upon methods of communication and coordination

- negotiation—mediation of conflict between the parents

- reattribution—challenging cognitive distortions about the relationship, reframing problems that are occurring

- work with children—helping the child(ren) to understand the transition and to externalize the conflict between his/her parents

- building parent–child understanding—how to help the child best function in the home.

Resources

- Bibliotherapy—there are many books and workbooks for children and teens regarding divorce

- Divorce Headquarters—online resource guide: www.divorcehq.com

- Children and Divorce: Helping Kids Cope with Separation and Divorce: www.helpguide.org/mental/children_divorce.htm

- Surviving Divorce: 20 Dos and Don'ts: www.huffingtonpost.com/2010/12/01/post_601_n_790653.html

Counselor Cautions

When working with children, especially adolescents, counselors should be aware of developmental periods in which the divorce has occurred (Gatins *et al.* 2013). This will assist in assessing whether the child's behavior is a result of adjustment difficulties following a divorce or if behavior is attributed to developmentally appropriate emotional and behavioral difficulties (Steinberg 2011).

Counselors should also be mindful of triangulation. Triangulation can occur when a family member does not directly communicate with another family member but will communicate with a third family member. Triangulation can occur not only between family members, but can also include the therapist. Counselors must be vigilant in recognizing and addressing triangulation in order to maintain neutrality.

Counselors have a duty to be knowledgeable about their state's laws and agency's policies regarding services requested by caregivers. Divorce cases where there is joint guardianship will likely require the signature of both parents. This can become problematic if there is one parent who does not agree with his/her child participating in treatment.

There may also be situations where counselors are asked for written recommendations regarding child custody. This may or may not be within the agency's mission or the counselor's expertise. Clear expectations should be discussed with parents regarding court testimonies and reports.

Discussion Questions

- What are your family's strengths?

- What's the best/worst thing about having two homes?

- What rules do you wish both homes had?

- How comfortable is it for everyone if you want to call Mom when you're at Dad's or want to call Dad when you're at Mom's?

- How are the transitions between parents' homes?

- What do you feel quality time is like with Mom? What about with Dad?

- Is there something that you do with Mom that you would like to start doing with Dad or something you do with Dad that you would like to start doing with Mom?

- What are the conversations like when Mom and Dad talk to one another?

- Do you ever feel put in the middle? How can you tell Mom/Dad when you are feeling this way?

- Are there any obstacles to having more fun together now? How could you overcome these?

- What friends or extended family members can all of you count on?

Ideas for Between-Session Homework

- Encourage a family dinner or a set family night at both homes.

- Assign the family a task of creating a manageable routine for transitioning back and forth between homes—ask the child (if age appropriate) to make a list of items that he/she would like to have at both homes, so as not to have to remember to take them back and forth every time.

- Ask the parents to create a manageable way to communicate. Ask them to think about how often they feel that it is necessary to communicate with one another as well as what types of situations may occur where they feel it is necessary to contact each other.

- Ask parents to look for books related to coping with/adjusting to divorce and read them to their children.

- Ask family members to identify hobbies that they enjoy or that they would like to try. Assign each member to participate in at least one hobby for the week.

- Ask the family to create a calendar to assist with creating a new routine. Include any activities the child participates in or events that the parent has to be at. Discuss finding a clear way to show what day the child will be at mom's and what day the child will be at dad's.

Therapeutic Activities

Activities included in this section are variations of evidenced-based practices tailored to be utilized with divorced families. Not all activities will apply to every family. Counselors should select those activities that best address a specific family's problem(s).

COMMUNICATION SHUTDOWN MATCHING GAME

PARTICIPANTS
Parents/caregivers only

PURPOSE
To enhance communication

MATERIALS

- Index cards
- Pen or pencil or markers

DESCRIPTION
Prior to the parents' arrival, write down several communication shutdown statements on index cards (several are listed below but be sure to use any specific ones that you have heard the parents using). Write each communication shutdown phrase *twice* on different index cards so that they are identical and can be used in a matching game. For example, if you have ten communication shutdown statements, you will have 20 index cards to be used in the game. If desired, similar statements can be written in the same color and differing statements can be written in different colors. Then explain to the parents/caregivers that communication shutdowns are those phrases that are likely to end any further reasonable discussion on a subject. Mix up the index cards and lay each card out on the table with the communication shutdowns facing down so they are hidden. Ask one parent to turn over two cards to find a match. If s/he did not find a match, it will be the other parent's turn. Don't forget to turn those cards back over so you cannot see the statements. If s/he did find matching statements, ask that parent to share her/his experiences and perceptions of this or similar statements and why

this could shut down communication. Continue until all the cards have been matched and discussed.

Here are some suggested communication shutdown statements (feel free to add or delete).

- Don't be ridiculous.

- That's not my responsibility.

- If it ain't broke, don't fix it.

- We tried that before and it didn't work.

- It simply can't be done.

- Let's get back to reality.

- Okay, but if it doesn't work, you're the one who's going to get the blame.

- Are you crazy?

DISCUSSION QUESTIONS

- What does it feel like to get "shut down"?

- Have you used any of these or similar kinds of communication shutdowns?

- What might happen if you stop using them?

- Why is it important to be able to communicate effectively with your former partner?

- Which one of you do you think will be the first one to work at changing bad communication habits?

GRIEVING WHAT USED TO BE

PARTICIPANTS
Children (ages 7–18)

PURPOSE
To grieve the loss of the intact family

MATERIALS

- Small boxes

- Paper cut into strips

- Pens or pencils

- Markers

DESCRIPTION

Explain to the family that while there may be advantages to a divorce (i.e. less conflict), children also need to grieve the loss of their former family. Then give each child a small box, several strips of paper, a pen or pencil and some markers. Instruct them to use the strips of paper to write down things that they will miss about having their parents together (one strip per grief item). Have them place these in their boxes as if the boxes were funeral caskets. If they would like, they can also decorate the "caskets" (boxes) in ways that represent saying goodbye. If time permits, the counselor and children can also have a "funeral" service for these items.

DISCUSSION QUESTIONS

- What were some of the things that you put in your "casket"? Of those, which will you miss the most?

- (If there is more than one child) In what ways were the things that you will miss similar or different from your siblings?

- How hard is it to say "goodbye" to these things?

- Does saying "goodbye" to these things mean that you will no longer have parents?

- In what ways are your parents still active in your lives?

- Do you think that the hurt that you feel now will always be there or will it get better?

- What are some ways that you can make yourself feel better when you are sad?

FEEL-OMETER

PARTICIPANTS

Parent/caregiver(s) and children (ages 5–14)

PURPOSE

To recognize and express feelings

MATERIALS

- Copies of Appendix C—Feelings Thermometers

- Crayons/markers

- A list of feelings words (i.e., sad, hurt, happy etc.)

DESCRIPTION

Prior to the session, make copies of Appendix C (Feelings Thermometers—Feel-ometers) so that each family member will each have a copy. Explain to family members that it can sometimes be hard to share our feelings with others, especially when we may not even be sure what our feelings are. Instruct family members to think of three situations where it was hard to tell others how they felt. This can be a situation that occurred at home or school—anywhere. Then ask family members to think of the three different feelings that they may have had during those times and to write them above each "Feel-ometer" on the page. (Younger family members may need assistance with writing the words. If family members have a difficult time thinking of feelings words, assist them by sharing a feelings words list.) Instruct family members to color in the level at which they felt those particular feelings on each thermometer.

DISCUSSION QUESTIONS

- What feeling was the highest on the "feel-ometer"? What was the lowest?
- How difficult was it for you to identify the *name* of the feeling that you were feeling?
- Have there been times when you couldn't describe how you were feeling? What did you do in those situations?
- Has anyone ever told you not to feel a certain way? What did you think of that?
- Who is someone in your family who you can talk to about your feelings? Who is someone outside your family who you can talk to about your feelings?

BACK AND FORTH

PARTICIPANTS
Parent/caregiver(s)* and children (ages 5–18)
*It is suggested that both parents be present for this activity. However, if only one parent is present, the activity can be modified by using the counselor or another family member to fill in as the other parent.

PURPOSE
To develop parent empathy for children

MATERIALS

- Backpack or some type of tote bag
- Items that you would travel with (i.e. clothing, toothbrush and paste, jacket, hairbrush, etc.)

DESCRIPTION
Prior to the session, spread the travel items all over one side of the room. Explain to parents that going back and forth between homes can be difficult for children. Instruct parents to stand on opposite sides of the room. Give the child (if more than one child is present they can take turns participating in the activity) the backpack/tote and direct her/him to stand next to the parent on the side of the room with the travel items. Explain to the family that every time you say, "Go" the child will load all of the travel items into the backpack/tote and walk across the room to the other parent and unload the items. Repeat "Go" several times allowing for less time each time that you say it.

Parents may help the child if s/he is on their side of the room. Stop the activity as the parents or child begin to look tired or frustrated.

DISCUSSION QUESTIONS

- What was it like carrying/loading/unloading your belongings? Did you want to say anything to your parents as you were doing it?

- *<To parent(s) only>* How did it feel to watch your child load/unload belongings?

- Is there currently a routine set up at home for days when transitioning between households? What is it? Is it working?

- If you do not already have a routine in place, what are some ideas for creating one?

- What other things might make transitions easier?

YOUR RULES VERSUS MY RULES

PARTICIPANTS
Parent/caregiver(s) only

PURPOSE
To identify frustrations in co-parenting and to "let go" of and accept differences in parenting

MATERIALS

- Paper
- Pens/pencils

DESCRIPTION
With the parents/caregivers, acknowledge that co-parenting after a divorce can be a challenge. Explain that although divorce has occurred, both parents continue to be linked through their children, although they may not always agree on parenting issues. While parents do not have to agree on everything regarding their children, they probably both agree that they share the goals of safety and well-being for their children. Hand each parent a piece of paper and a pen or pencil. Ask them to each create a list of things that the other parent does, or permits, that s/he does *not* agree with. When the lists are completed, do *not* let parents read them out loud. Instruct them each to select two items from their lists that they would be willing to let go of (to simply accept and not try to change). Ask them to share these briefly. Then ask them each to read out the *one* item from their lists that they are most concerned about, and assist them in negotiating these items. Keep the focus on problem-solving and not on the history of the problem.

DISCUSSION QUESTIONS

- Was it difficult to determine what you were going to "let go" of?

- How did you determine that these were things that you could "let go" of?

- How did it feel to "let it go?"

- How hard will it be for you to truly let those things go? Will you take them back or really let them go?

- What does it mean to "agree to disagree"? What would it mean for the two of you?

- Why is it okay for rules and expectations to vary from house to house?

MY SUPERHERO CAPE

PARTICIPANTS

Children (ages 4–10)

PURPOSE

To develop coping skills

MATERIALS

- Bath towels

- Construction paper

- Markers

- Glue

- Scissors

- Glitter (optional)

DESCRIPTION

Begin the session by asking the children what superheroes they are familiar with. Prompt their discussion with questions about superheroes, including: what does a superhero do? How does a superhero act? Who does a superhero help? Explain to the children that our coping skills are like superheroes. They help us when we are scared or need help. Then ask the children to name some coping skills (i.e. taking a deep breath, taking a time out, exercising, talking to someone, journaling, etc.). Direct them each to select a different coping skill and to decorate a bath towel as that coping skill/superhero cape. If there is time, allow the children to wear their capes and "fly" around the room extolling the virtues and strengths of that particular coping skill.

DISCUSSION QUESTIONS

- What superhero/coping skills did we have here today? Are there others?

- Which of these superhero/coping skills have "rescued" you from stress before? How did you use it?

- Which superhero/coping skills are new to you? Would you ever try them?

- What parts of your parents' divorce need you to call on your superhero/coping skill?

- Are there other stressful situations in your life where you could use any of these superhero/coping skills?

- How can you remember to use your coping skills?

- Is there anyone who can help you remember them?

IT'S NOT MY FAULT

PARTICIPANTS
Parent/caregiver(s) and children (ages 5–18)

PURPOSE
To reduce irrational child guilt

MATERIALS

- None

DESCRIPTION
Explain to family members that children often irrationally believe that the divorce was their fault. They blame themselves for all kinds of reasons—because they didn't do their chores, because they complained to one parent about the other, because they didn't behave well enough, etc. Tell the children that you would like them to create a rap about the divorce not being their fault. Parents may assist if children invite them to participate. After the rap is created, ask the children to perform it in front of the adults. Every child should have a part in the performance.

DISCUSSION QUESTIONS

- In what ways have your brains tried to trick you into believing that the divorce was your fault?

- Do you believe the words of your rap?

- Is it good to hear out loud that it's not your fault?

- Has anyone told you that the divorce is not your fault? Did you believe her/him?

- If it wasn't your fault (and it wasn't!), why do you think your mom and dad got a divorce?

DEAR MOM AND/OR DAD

PARTICIPANTS
Children (ages 6–15)

PURPOSE
To increase children's separation from parental conflict

MATERIALS

- Paper
- Pen or pencil

DESCRIPTION
Explain to the children that parents sometimes are so angry with each other that they use the kids to pass messages back and forth to each other, or they badmouth the other parent. Explain that children need to remind parents not to involve them in their conflicts—and they may need to remind them of this more than once! One way to help children separate from their parents' conflict is to have them write a letter to Mom, Dad or both of them. In order to prompt a thorough and assertive message in the letter, it can be helpful to have a template with blank spaces to fill in. The example below is not meant to be used precisely as written, but it can give counselors an idea for how to set up a template.

Dear Mom/Dad,

This is my formal resignation from _____. While I understand that _____, I no longer can _____ because it makes me feel _____.

   Also, I would appreciate it if you would _____. I love you and I want to please you, but it is not good for me to _____ any longer. I know that you will understand.

   This is my only childhood. I know that you would want _____ for me. Thanks so much for your attention to this. I love you.

Signed,

_____

DISCUSSION QUESTIONS

- How do you feel now that you have written this letter to your parent(s)?
- Do you think you will give it to them/her/him? When?

- What do you think their reaction will be to the letter?

- If your parent(s) forgets about the letter and continues to make you feel uncomfortable, what can you say to them/her/him?

- How can you make sure that you are respectful to your parent(s) while letting them know what you don't like?

LINKS TO "CHAIN"GE

PARTICIPANTS
Parent/caregiver(s) and children (ages 7–18)

PURPOSE
To re-establish/create positive relationships among family members, increasing cohesion

MATERIALS

- Construction paper (cut into strips—enough for each participant to have five different colored strips of paper)

- Tape

- Scissors

DESCRIPTION
Discuss with family members the importance of recognizing strengths—individual strengths and collective strengths. Explain that when people face adversity it is often their shared strengths that help them overcome it. Provide each family member with five different colored strips of construction paper. Make sure that everyone has the same five colors. Instruct them to write down the following on their strips of construction paper.

- Color #1—Something that I do well that, if I do more of it, will help my family.

- Color #2—Something that I appreciate about my family as a whole.

- Color #3—Someone outside of our family who supports us.

- Color #4—Good ways that I handle stress.

- Color #5—Something tough that I overcame or handled well.

Then direct the family to make a paper chain starting with one family member and then going around the room so that each person adds a link one at a time. (Links are created by taking a strip of paper, forming it into a circle and taping the ends together; then putting another strip of paper through the first loop, forming another loop and taping the ends.) Ask family members to say out loud what they wrote on the link as it is being added to the chain. Continue this process until the chain is complete.

DISCUSSION QUESTIONS

- How does it feel to hear all the strengths of your family?
- Did you learn anything new about your family from this activity?
- Can you think of other strengths that each of you has that didn't get included in the chain? Would you like to add those to your chain now?
- How can these strengths help you adjust to the divorce?
- How can these strengths help you with other stressors?
- What are some ways that you can remind each other of the strengths of your family?

OH, HOW WE SAY THINGS!

PARTICIPANTS
Parent/caregiver(s) and children (ages 10–18)

PURPOSE
To improve communication

MATERIALS

- Dry erase board or flip chart
- Markers
- Paper
- Pens or pencils

DESCRIPTION
Prior to the family's arrival, write the following statements on a dry erase board or flip chart.

A) Statement indicating surprise.

B) Statement indicating that we will be doing some other kind of shopping.

C) Statement indicating that we are not going at this time but might go at another time.

D) Statement indicating some other group will be shopping today.

E) Statement indicating we absolutely will not be shopping today.

Explain to the family that voice inflections are a major part of verbal communication and that people need to be aware of how they say things in order to communicate their *intended* meaning. Direct the family to write the numbers one to five in a column (as if they were going to take a spelling test). Explain that you will be reading the sentence, "We are not going grocery shopping today," using five different inflections that represent the five different meanings on the dry erase board (or flip chart). The family should write the letter that corresponds to the meaning from the dry erase board (or flip chart) each time that you read the statement.

Read the sentence five times, emphasizing the words in bold.

1. "**We** are not going grocery shopping today." (answer = D)
2. "We are not going grocery shopping today**?**" (answer = A)
3. "We are **not** going grocery shopping today." (answer = E)
4. "We are not going **grocery** shopping today." (answer = B)
5. "We are not going grocery shopping **today**." (answer = C)

DISCUSSION QUESTIONS

- Were you surprised that the same statement could have so many different meanings?
- What do you think this says about communication?
- Do you have any examples of when you intended one message but another person heard it differently?
- What do you think your greatest communication struggles are?
- What are some ways that you can work on this?

Additional Activities That May be Helpful

- Guilt Gobblers in Chapter 3: Single-Parent Families with an Absent Parent (p.29)
- The Feelings Game in Chapter 7: Families with an Incarcerated Loved One (p.91)
- Compliment Hot Seat in Chapter 7: Families with an Incarcerated Loved One (p.95)
- Reflecting, Reflecting, Reflecting in Chapter 7: Families with an Incarcerated Loved One (p.96)
- Round Robin "I" Statements in Chapter 8: Families with a Substance-Abusing Child (p.114)
- Difficult Feelings in Chapter 9: Families with Parent Substance Abuse (p.126) A Bag of Coping in Chapter 10: Families with a Mentally Ill Parent (p.148)
- No More Stinkin' Thinkin' in Chapter 11: Families with a Chronically Ill Child (p.156)

References

American Psychological Association (APA) (2013) *Marriage and Divorce.* Washington: American Psychological Association. Available at www.apa.org/topics/divorce/index.aspx, accessed on 3 October 2013.

Appell, J. (2006) *Divorce Doesn't Have to be That Way: A Handbook for the Helping Professional.* Atascadero, CA: Impact Publishers.

Berman, W.H. (1988) "The relationship of ex-spouse attachment to adjustment following divorce." *Journal of Family Psychology 1,* 3, 312–328.

Bottom, T.L. (2013) "The well-being of divorced fathers: a review and suggestions for future research." *Journal of Divorce and Remarriage 54,* 3, 214–230.

Braver, S.L. and Griffin, W.A. (2000) "Engaging fathers in the post-divorce family." *Marriage and Family Review 29,* 4, 247–267.

Centers for Disease Control and Prevention National Vital Statistics System (2011) *Marriage and Divorces.* Available at www.cdc.gov/nchs/mardiv.htm, accessed on 19 July 2013.

Dozier, B. (2004) *Two Home Families: A Family Systems Approach to Divorce Therapy.* Bloomington, IN: iUniverse Inc.

Emery, R. (1994) *Renegotiating Family Relationships.* New York: Guilford Press.

Gatins, D., Kinlaw, C.R. and Dunlap, L.L. (2013) "Do the kids think they're okay? Adolescents' view on the impact of marriage and divorce." *Journal of Divorce and Remarriage 54,* 4, 313–328.

Heatherington, M. (2002) *For Better or for Worse: Divorce Reconsidered.* New York, NY: Norton.

Isaacs, M.B., Montalvo, B. and Abelsohn, D. (2000) *Therapist of the Difficult Divorce: Managing Crisis, Reorienting Warring Couples, Working with the Children, and Expediting Court Processes.* Northval, NJ: Book-Mart Press.

Iowa State University (1996) *Divorce Matters: Coping with Stress and Change.* Iowa: Iowa State University. Available at www.extension.iastate.edu/Publications/PM1637.pdf, accessed on 3 October 2013.

Kelly, J.B. (2000) "Children's adjustment in conflicted marriage and divorce: a decade review of research." *Journal of the American Academy of Child Psychiatry 39,* 8, 963–973.

Kitson, G.C. (1992) *Portrait of Divorce: Adjustment to Marital Breakdown.* New York: Guilford.

Kposowa, A.J. (2003) "Divorce and suicide risk." *Journal of Epidemiology and Community Health 57,* 993.

Laasko, J.H. and Adams, S. (2006) "Noncustodial fathers' involvement with their children: a right or a privilege?" *Families in Society 87,* 1, 85–94.

Lebow, J. (2003) "Integrative family therapy for disputes involving child custody and visitation." *Journal of Family Psychology 19,* 2, 181–192.

Steinberg, L. (2011) *Adolescence* (9th edition). New York, NY: McGraw-Hill.

Trust (2013) *Divorce Rates in 2013: A Look Forward and a Look Back.* Available at www.trustmattersmost.com/news/divorce-rates-in-2013-a-look-forward-and-a-look-back, accessed on 3 October 2013.

Wallerstein, J.S. and Blakeslee, S. (1996) *Second Chances.* Chicago, IL: Houghton Mifflin.

Weiss, R.S. (1975) *Marital Separation.* New York: Basic Books.

CHAPTER 5

Blended Families

Introduction

Half of all marriages each year are remarriages, and 65 percent of these remarriages include children from a previous marriage (Chadwick and Heaton 1999). Blended families represent a unique and complex family system in their composition, structure and development (Furrow and Palmer 2007). The composition of blended families consists of remarried couples and can include their own biological children as well as children from previous relationships who may or may not reside in the home. The age ranges of these children can vary widely. This complexity can create a conflict, which is why many blended families seek treatment within the first four years of the remarriage (Pasley *et al.* 1996). Blended family types include:

- only one member of the couple has prior child/children

- both members of the couple have at least one pre-existing child

- only one member has one or more prior children and the couple have another child together

- both members of the couple have prior children and the couple have another child together.

Other variations can include:

- children living with the couple

- children visiting the couple

- other biological parent actively involved

- other biological parent not involved.

Potential Challenges/Vulnerabilities

Blended families are more vulnerable than first-time marriages, as evidenced by higher divorce rates compared with first-time marriages (Kurdek 1991; O'Connor *et al.* 1999). Entering into a marriage with children from a previous relationship can quickly produce tension and conflict based on differing expectations and conflicting loyalties. Parents do not always recognize that just because they fell in love and chose to marry one another, this is no guarantee that they will love each other's children (Hayes and Hayes 1986; Walsh 1992).

Conflicts over discipline and childrearing rank first on the list of problems in remarriages (Kupisch 1987; Maddox 1975; McClenahan 1978; Messinger 1976; Visher and Visher 1979; Walsh 1992). Stepparents may not recognize that they are not a replacement parent but rather a new addition to the family. Biological parents may have become more lenient due to the guilt of the divorce and stepparents may want to step in too early to take over discipline.

Children may resent the new stepparent or feel guilty if they like their new stepparent. There may also be grief around the loss of the biological parent or the former family unit. Hayes and Hayes (1986) found that members of blended families must resolve their losses associated with a divorce as a prelude to creating a successful blended family.

Sibling rivalries are common in any family and traditionally territorial battles are resolved on the basis of age privilege. However, with a blended family, this hierarchy is unclear and may result in additional sibling disputes (Walsh 1992). This rivalry becomes even more intense if any of the stepsiblings have unresolved anger about the separation and divorce (Wallerstein and Kelly 1980).

Strengths

Blended families have the potential to create a more positive living environment than the previous conflictual family life. The change can create another learning environment regarding healthy family relationships for the children. Having two families can "broaden your horizons." Positive bonds with stepparents can also create greater appreciation and value for relationships that are not strictly based upon blood relation.

There are additional extended kinships that have the potential to evolve into positive relationships for all family members. There have been consistent findings in research that remarried individuals who maintain moderate levels of contact with extended family members exhibit better marital quality (Clingempeel 1981; Goetting 1981; Skeen, Covi and Robinson 1985; Walsh 1992; White 1982).

Finally, remarriage can provide a more stable financial situation. A single parent providing for her/his children on one income would likely benefit from having an additional income to contribute to the family's needs.

Empirical Support for Treatment

Research suggests that the characteristics of successful blended families include creating and maintaining a solid group identity as a family (Banker *et al.* 2004), reducing inter-group biases (Banker and Gaertner 1998) and engaging in marital and parental role negotiation (Bray 1999; Stewart 2005). Additionally, as with all couples, communication skills (Portrie and Hill 2005) and conflict and stress management (Crosbie-Burnett 1989) are important.

Clinical approaches that support successful blended families include:

- processing the past and present emotional experience of family members to find a "middle ground" and foster a new family identity

- clarifying boundaries within the remarried family, particularly around co-parenting

- allowing for grief work, particularly as children mourn the distance of a previous custodial parent, and the loss of a previous extended family and the hope that one day reconciliation and reunion would occur

- integrating the differing developmental needs (Furrow and Palmer 2007; Pasley et al. 1996; Riches and Dawson 2001).

Emotionally Focused Family Therapy (EFFT) offers a unique approach designed to promote the development of secure emotional connections between blended family members. EFFT includes: validating and normalizing family members' individual emotional experience; reframing presenting problems; identifying and de-escalating any negative interactions, both within and between the biological families and stepfamilies; facilitating the expression of attachment needs between biological parents and children; and clarifying the relationship expectations between stepparents and stepchildren (Furrow and Palmer 2007).

Resources

- Guide to Step-parenting and Blended Families: www.helpguide.org/mental/blended_families_stepfamilies.htm

- National Stepfamily Resource Center: www.stepfamilies.info

- Band Back Together: www.bandbacktogether.com/blended-families-resources

- Blended Family Support Network: Equipping Stepfamilies Worldwide for Success: www.blendedfamilyfocus.com/resources

Counselor Cautions

Counselors should make sure they honor the integrity and identity of the stepfamily by focusing on the stepfamily system (Visher and Visher 1996). While one cannot dismiss the influence of an ex-spouse, the therapeutic relationship is with the new family system.

Counselors should be alert to triangulation within the family, especially if there is limited interaction between biological parents, or if there is a conflicted relationship between stepchildren and their stepparents. The ability to recognize and address these issues is imperative to healthy family functioning. Counselors should also be able to identify when *they* are being triangulated, to avoid being "sucked in" to taking sides.

Discussion Questions

- What was the hardest thing to get used to when your family first blended? What was the easiest?

- What rules do you have now that you didn't have before?

- How comfortable are you with what you call your stepparent?

- Do you feel guilty for showing affection to your stepparent?

- How are the transitions between parents' homes?

- Is there something that you feel would make the transition easier?

- What is your reaction to seeing your child engaged and affectionate with someone other than yourself?

- Do you ever wish that things could go back to the way they were before? Do you have any questions about the divorce that you feel will help you better understand/deal with the separation?

- What do you enjoy most about having new brothers/sisters? The least?

Ideas for Between-Session Homework

- Ask the family to develop a new family ritual. This should be something that they do weekly. For example, family games night, family dinner, taking a walk in the evenings, etc.

- If transition between homes is an issue, assign the family a task of creating a manageable routine for transitioning back and forth. This can include setting up specific and consistent pick up and drop off times, as well as making sure they assist the child in developing a routine of what they are going to take with them.

- Ask the family to create and maintain a calendar. With blended families it is likely that activities are going to increase and it may be a challenge to keep everything straight.

- Encourage the family to have a family meeting at the beginning of each week. This time can be utilized to discuss the calendar for the week, taking time to make sure that everyone knows where they need to be and when, what parent/stepparent is picking up or dropping off and what items are needed for the activity.

- Encourage communication between biological parents and stepparents. This helps them to present a united front and decreases the possibility of triangulation.

- Encourage the couple to establish a date night, explaining that it will help to keep their marriage healthy.

Therapeutic Activities

Activities included in this section are variations of evidenced-based practices tailored to be utilized with blended families. Not all activities will apply to every family. Counselors should select those activities that best address a specific family's problem(s).

MERGING CARS

PARTICIPANTS

Parent/caregiver(s) and children (ages 4–10)

PURPOSE

To normalize the difficulties of accepting new family members

MATERIALS

- Drawing or play mat of a road
- Several toy cars

DESCRIPTION

Explain to family members how difficult it is for already existing families to allow "newcomers" in. Then set up the "road" so that several cars are lined up "bumper to bumper" with one car attempting to merge into the roadway. Allow each family member to have a turn trying to "merge" the outside car, moving and adjusting the cars to allow room.

DISCUSSION QUESTIONS

- What must a merging car be cautious of? What must the other cars on the road do in order to allow the merging car in? Who has the tougher job?
- What happens if the cars on the road do not let the merging car in?
- What are the merging car's frustrations?
- What is the worst thing that could happen with merging cars? What is the best thing that could happen?
- How is this like your family? Have you allowed your new stepparent to "merge" into the family?
- What other thoughts do you have about this activity?

CREATING CONNECTION

PARTICIPANTS

Stepparent and one child (ages 12–18)

PURPOSE

To increase communication and cooperation

MATERIALS

- Paper
- Crayon or markers

DESCRIPTION

Explain to family members that it can be difficult for two people to get to know one another when surrounded by others. Provide the two family members with one sheet of paper. Direct them to jointly make a decision about what kind of picture to draw together and then ask them to go ahead and draw it.

DISCUSSION QUESTIONS

- How difficult/easy was it to make a decision together about what to draw? What strategies did you use in order to agree?
- How difficult/easy was it to draw together? What accommodations did you have to make for one another as you drew?
- What was enjoyable about the activity? What was stressful about the activity?
- How was this activity similar to your relationship at home? How was it different?
- What strategies did you use in this activity that might be helpful at home?

GET ACQUAINTED

PARTICIPANTS

Parent/caregiver(s) and children (ages 5–18)

PURPOSE

To increase communication

MATERIALS

- Paper (can be cut to allow for less waste)
- Dark colored marker
- Tape

DESCRIPTION

Prior to the family's arrival, write the following words on separate pieces of paper and tape them around the room (include the words that you feel best fit the family that you are working with – if you feel that some do not relate to the family then do not include them).

- Trust
- Being together
- Money
- Time
- Love
- Freedom
- Space
- Fun
- Anger
- School
- Each other
- Death
- Failing
- Fighting
- Understanding
- Games
- Movies
- Television
- Respect
- Encouragement
- Laughter
- Hugs

Explain to family members that day-to-day life can make it difficult to communicate on a deeper level. Families get so busy that they do not always express their thoughts, feelings, wants, etc. Tell family members that you are going to read various statements one at a time (see example statements below) and then they should stand by a word taped to the wall that best describes what their response is.

1. One thing that is important to me is…
2. One thing our family needs is…

3. One thing I don't care about is…

4. One thing I want is…

5. One thing I worry about is…

6. One thing I wish we had is…

7. One thing that makes me happy is…

8. The hardest thing for me to do is…

DISCUSSION QUESTIONS

- What are some things you learned about your family members?

- Did you notice any similarities?

- Do you have any questions for one another based on the responses you saw?

- Are there other words that came to mind that you thought would have been a better choice?

- How easy or difficult is it for you to express your feelings at home?

- What are some ways that you can become more comfortable with expressing how you feel?

SCULPTING

PARTICIPANTS

Parent/caregiver(s) and children (ages 5–18)

PURPOSE

To increase positive communication and acknowledgement of strengths

MATERIALS

- Play-Doh (one pot per person)

- Paper

- Pen or pencils

DESCRIPTION

Discuss with family members how it can be difficult to pick out the positive things about our family members, especially when we're not getting along. Ask family members to sit at a table with a piece of paper and a can of Play-Doh in front of them. Instruct family members to write their name on their piece of paper. (This will help the family to remember whose sculpture they are working on.) Instruct family members to create a sculpture of her/himself (allow approximately three to five minutes) and to place it on their piece of paper. Once they are complete, ask everyone to move one seat to their right. Instruct them to change the sculpture in some small way to symbolize something that they like or appreciate about that particular family member. Ask family members to describe what they changed and why. Continue the rotation until all family members are back to their original sculpture.

DISCUSSION QUESTIONS

- How did it feel to hear positive things about you?
- How did it feel to share your positive things about your family members?
- How often do family members give one another compliments or express appreciation?
- Did you see something that someone else changed that you would like to talk about?
- What do you think that the purpose of this activity was?

LAY IT ALL OUT

PARTICIPANTS

Parent/caregiver(s) only

PURPOSE

To examine unspoken expectations

MATERIALS

- Paper
- Pens or pencils

DESCRIPTION

Explain to the parent/stepparent(s) that when entering into a blended family everyone has expectations that often do not get verbally expressed. This can cause conflict and create triangulation in the home. Provide each person with a sheet of paper and a pen or pencil. Ask them to write down expectations that they have for one another in the following areas: discipline; household duties; parent duties. Add any other areas that may pertain to this couple's needs. Once this is complete, allow the couple to share their list one at a time. Ask the listening individual to keep all questions and comments to her/himself until the speaker has finished. Then facilitate a discussion of what may be realistic and unrealistic expectations.

DISCUSSION QUESTIONS

- Did you have any similarities on your lists?
- What expectations did you list that your spouse is already doing?

- What expectations did you hear from your spouse that you were surprised about or were new to you?

- Did you leave anything off your list because you were fearful it would anger your spouse?

- Which expectation is the most important to you? Which could you give up?

SNOOPY SIBLINGS

PARTICIPANTS
Children (ages 7–18) only

PURPOSE
To increase cohesion between stepsiblings

MATERIALS

- Paper

- Pens or pencils

DESCRIPTION
The session will require a homework "assignment" *prior* to the session. At the end of the family session prior to this activity, you should assign siblings to "snoop" on one another during the week. Explain to them that the "rules" are they cannot invade each other's personal boundaries while gathering their information. They should look for their siblings' likes/dislikes/favorite activities, objects, relationships, etc.

In this session provide each sibling with a sheet of paper and a pen or pencil. Instruct siblings to make the same number of columns on the page as there are children in the room (i.e. two children will make two columns; three children will make three columns). Direct them to write "Me" at the top of one column and the name(s) of their sibling(s) at the top of the other column(s). Then ask them to write the numbers one to ten down the side of each column. Explain that you will read a statement and they should write what their response is under "Me," and what they think their siblings' responses will be under their name. Once all the statements are read, siblings should check their answers to see how many they got correct.

Example statements:

1. Favorite food

2. Favorite show

3. Least favorite chore

4. Best friend

5. Favorite day of the week

6. Least favorite subject in school

7. Favorite subject in school

8. Favorite activity

9. Favorite family activity

10. Something that makes you happy

DISCUSSION QUESTIONS

- What did you learn about your sibling that you didn't know before this activity?

- Was there anything about your sibling that surprised you?

- Did you notice any similarities between each other?

- Did you have fun participating in the activity throughout the week?

- Is there something that your sibling does that you would like to know more about?

- What are some things that you and your sibling can do together?

EXPRESSION COLLAGE

PARTICIPANTS

Parent/caregiver(s) and children (ages 5–18)

PURPOSE

To increase communication

MATERIALS

- One large poster board

- Magazines

- Scissors

- Glue sticks

DESCRIPTION

Explain to family members that change is difficult and that everyone handles it differently. Talk about how change can stir up negative as well as positive feelings, but negative feelings do not last forever. Explain that talking about feelings can allow opportunities to address miscommunications or misunderstandings. Instruct family members to cut out words or images that describe how they feel about their family life. Family members should then glue their cutouts onto the poster board creating a collage. Do not allow criticism of each other's choices of cutouts.

DISCUSSION QUESTIONS

- How difficult was it to pick something that described how you felt about your family life?
- What do you notice about the collage?
- Is there something on the collage that you want to know more about?
- Is there an image or word on the collage that you would not have chosen?
- Pick one thing that you cut out and tell us why you chose that image/word.

MY "I JUST WANT TO SCREAM!" BOX

PARTICIPANTS
Parent/caregiver(s) and children (ages 5–18)

PURPOSE
To increase coping

MATERIALS

- Empty cereal boxes (one per family member)
- Paper towel tube (one per family member)
- Tape
- Scrap paper or old newspaper
- Scissors
- Magazines
- Crayons or markers
- Construction paper

DESCRIPTION
Explain to family members that experiencing grief is not just something that happens when there is a death. Grief is a feeling that can occur with any type of loss, such as a loss of time with a non-custodial parent, or the loss of the hope that parents will be back together, etc. Grief can cause several different types of emotions, one of which is anger. Provide each family member with a cereal box, a paper towel tube and scrap paper. Tell family members that they can decorate their cereal boxes however they would like—that it can be a representation of all the things that cause them to feel angry. Then instruct family members to crumple the scrap paper and stuff it inside their cereal box. Close the lid and cut a hole in the top of it so that the paper towel tube can be inserted (therapists may have to assist younger children with cutting). Next, insert the paper towel tube into the hole and tape it to the cereal box in order to secure it. Tell everyone to scream into their boxes.

DISCUSSION QUESTIONS

- When was a time that you were angry and didn't know how to express your anger?

- What are some other things that you can do when you are angry/sad/frustrated?

- Can you share with us one thing on your box and explain why you chose that image/word/drawing?

- What did you notice about other family members' boxes?

- What is one thing that you can do to help a family member with their anger/sadness? What is something that you would like someone to do for you?

R-E-S-P-E-C-T

PARTICIPANTS

Parent/caregiver(s) only

PURPOSE

To increase respect and communication between stepparents and biological parents

MATERIALS

- White board or flip chart

- Dry erase markers

DESCRIPTION

Begin the activity with a discussion on the definition of respect. Explain that although we may have anger and frustration towards our child/ren's or stepchild/ren's biological parent, it is important to respect her/him in order for children to have a positive adjustment. On the white board (or flip chart) ask parents to write words that they feel represent respect. Once complete, ask the parent/stepparent to rate themselves on a scale of one to ten (one = poor; ten = excellent) on each word based on how they have behaved towards the identified biological parent.

DISCUSSION QUESTIONS

- What would you say your average score was? Is this acceptable to you?

- How could you increase your score?

- Why do you think it's important to have respect for your child's or stepchild's other parent?

- Does one have to receive respect in order to give respect?

- When is it most difficult for you to respect your child's or stepchild's other parent? Are there ways you can prepare for this?

RULES

PARTICIPANTS
Parent/caregiver(s) and children (ages 4–18)

PURPOSE
To establish boundaries and consistency

MATERIALS
- Large poster board
- Markers

DESCRIPTION
Talk to family members about the fact that when joining with another family, there are going to be times where things are confusing. What may have been a rule in one family may not be a rule in another family. As part of creating a new family identity, rules and boundaries must be agreed upon and applied to everyone equally. On one side of the poster board write "Rules" and on the other "Consequences." Ask family members to name some rules that they feel should be part of the household. (The family can take turns writing, or you can assign someone to write.) Then, for each rule, ask the family to identify a consequence if that rule is broken.

DISCUSSION QUESTIONS
- *<To children only>* What rules are on the chart that were not rules for you before?
- Are there any rules that should be added?
- Why do families have rules?
- *<To parent(s) only>* How well do you think you will be able to enforce the consequences? Why are consequences necessary? Does a parent have to be angry in order to enforce consequences or can they be enforced with empathy? How would one enforce a consequence with empathy?
- *<To children only>* How easy/hard will it be to follow the rules? What would help you to follow the rules?

Additional Activities That May be Helpful

- Mother, May I? in Chapter 3: Single-Parent Families with an Absent Parent (p.25)
- Paper Stack in Chapter 3: Single-Parent Families with an Absent Parent (p.26)
- Family Shield in Chapter 3: Single-Parent Families with an Absent Parent (p.28)

- Sweet Sentiments in Chapter 3: Single-Parent Families with an Absent Parent (p.30)

- Grieving What Used to Be in Chapter 4: Divorced/Separated/Unmarried Families—Both parents available (p.41)

- Your Rules versus My Rules in Chapter 4: Divorced/Separated/Unmarried Families—Both parents available (p.44)

- Round Robin "I" Statements in Chapter 8: Families with a Substance-Abusing Child (p.114)

- Couple's Communication Poker in Chapter 9: Families with Parent Substance Abuse (p.133)

- A Bag of Coping in Chapter 10: Families with a Mentally Ill Parent (p.148)

References

Banker, B.S. and Gaertner, S.L. (1998) "Achieving stepfamily harmony: an intergroup-relations approach." *Journal of Family Psychology 12*, 3, 310–325.

Banker, B.S., Gaertner, S.L., Dovidio, J.F., Houlette, M., Johnson, K.M. and Riek, B.M. (2004) "Reducing Stepfamily Conflict: The Importance of Inclusive Identity." In M. Bennett and F. Sani (eds) *The Development of the Social Self.* New York: Psychology Press.

Bray, J. (1999) "From Marriage to Remarriage and Beyond: Findings From the Developmental Issues in Stepfamilies Research Project." In E. M. Hetherington (ed.) *Coping with Divorce, Single Parenting, and Remarriage: A Risk and Resiliency Perspective.* Mahwah, NJ: Lawrence Erlbaum Associates.

Chadwick, B.A. and Heaton, T. B. (1999) *Statistical Handbook on the American Family* (2nd edition). Phoenix: Oryx.

Clingempeel, W.G. (1981) "Quasi-kin relationships and marital quality in stepfather families." *Journal of Personality and Social Psychology 41*, 890–901.

Crosbie-Burnett, M. (1989) "Application of family stress theory to remarriage: A model for assessing and helping stepfamilies." *Family Relations 38*, 323–331.

Furrow, J. and Palmer, G. (2007) "EFFT and blended families: Building bonds from the inside out." *Journal of Systemic Therapies 26*, 4, 44–58.

Goetting, A. (1981) "Divorce outcome research." *Journal of Family Issues 2*, 350–378.

Hayes, R.L. and Hayes, B.A. (1986) "Remarriage families: counseling parents, stepparents, and their children." *Counseling and Human Development 18*, 1–8.

Kupisch, S. (1987) "Children and Stepfamilies." In A. Thomas and J. Grimes (eds) *Children's Needs: Psychological Perspectives.* Washington, DC: National Association of Psychologists.

Kurdek, L.A. (1991) "Marital stability and changes in marital quality in newly wed couples: a test of the contextual model." *Journal of Social and Personal Relationships 8*, 27–48.

Maddox, B. (1975) *The Half-parent.* New York: New American Library.

McClenahan, C. (1978) *Group Work with Stepparents and their Spouses.* Unpublished manuscript.

Messinger, L. (1976) "Remarriage between divorced people with children from previous marriages." *Journal of Marriage and Family Counseling 2*, 193–200.

O'Connor, T.G., Pickering, K., Dunn, J. and Golding, J. (1999) "Frequency and predictors of relationship dissolutions in a community sample in England." *Journal of Family Psychology 13*, 443–449.

Pasley, K., Roden, K. Visher, E.B. and Visher, J. (1996) "Successful stepfamily therapy: client perspectives." *Journal of Marital and Family Therapy 22*, 343–358.

Portrie, T. and Hill, N. (2005) "Blended families: a critical review of the current research." *The Family Journal: Counseling and Therapy for Couples and Families 13*, 4, 445–451.

Riches, G. and Dawson, P. (2001) "Daughters' dilemmas: grief resolution whose widowed fathers remarry early." *Journal of Family Therapy 22*, 360–374.

Skeen, P., Covi, R.B. and Robinson, B.E. (1985) "Stepfamilies: a review of the literature with suggestion for practitioners." *Journal of Counseling and Development 64*, 121–125.

Stewart, S.D. (2005) "Boundary ambiguity in stepfamilies." *Journal of Family Issues 26*, 7, 1002–1029.

Visher, E.B. and Visher, J.S. (1979) *Stepfamilies: A Guide to Working with Stepparents and Stepchildren.* New York: Brunner/Mazel.

Visher, J.S. and Visher, E.B. (1996) *Therapy with Stepfamilies.* New York: Brunner/Maze.

Wallerstein, J.S. and Kelly, J.B. (1980) *Surviving the Break-up: How Children Actually Cope with Divorce.* New York: Basic Books.

Walsh, W.M. (1992) "Twenty major issues in remarriage families." *Journal of Counseling and Development 70*, 709–715.

White, K.R. (1982) "The relationship between socioeconomic status and academic achievement." *Psychological Bulletin 91*, 481–488.

CHAPTER 6

Families with Grandparents as Caregivers

Introduction

Grandparents as "parents," or grandfamilies, are a growing group. In 2010 there were 2.7 million grandparents in the United States who reported that they were responsible for the basic needs of one or more grandchildren under 18 years of age. Of these caregivers, 1.7 million were grandmothers and 1 million were grandfathers (US Census Bureau 2010). Approximately 38.5 percent of these grandparents have had their grandkids for more than five years (US Census Bureau 2008).

Despite growing numbers of grandfamilies among Caucasians, a disproportionate number of African American and Hispanic grandparents are primary caregivers for grandchildren (Fuller-Thomson and Minkler 2000). Approximately 40 percent of African American grandparents live with two or more grandchildren (Mutchler, Lee and Baker 2003). African American grandfamilies mostly consist of grandmother-only headed families, whereas Hispanic grandfamilies tend to have both grandmother and grandfather (Goodman and Silverstein 2002).

Grandparents may become primary caregivers for numerous reasons: parental death, parental abandonment, parental incarceration, abuse/neglect resulting in the child/ren being removed from the home, or parental physical or mental illness. Researchers have reported that there is a rise in grandparents taking over parenting roles. These factors include: parental alcohol and drug abuse, HIV/AIDS, the incarceration of women, divorce and teenage pregnancy (Harrison, Richman and Vittimberga 2000; Burnette 1997; Caliandro and Hughes 1998; Dressel and Barnhill 1994; Goodman and Silverstein 2002; Jendrek 1994; Joslin and Brouard 1995; Minkler and Roe 1993, Longoria 2009).

Potential Challenges/Vulnerabilities

Grandparents who have taken on primary parenting roles can experience caregiver burden. Caregiver burden refers to high levels of stress due to caring for another person(s). It includes physical, psychological, emotional, social and financial stressors (Dowdell 2004; Chou 2000; Davidhizar, Bechtel and Woodring 2000; DesRoches *et al.* 2002; Grinstead *et al.* 2003). After years of not having to care for young children, these grandparents are faced with the demands of childcare, school work, after-school activities, transportation, etc. Grandparents may also experience conflicting feelings regarding their own child's inability to adequately parent.

Approximately 33 percent of children referred for counseling services due to behavioral problems are living with grandparents (Grant 2000). However, this is misleading as these children often experience parent abandonment and/or negative parent–child relationships, which contribute to behavioral problems. There may also be grief issues for children who have been removed from their nuclear family. This may also be true for the grandparent, who has lost his/her own child.

Because grandparent households are likely a result of a crisis, there is a high probability that the grandparent(s) were not expecting their new role and lacked time for adequate preparation. Caregiving responsibilities are also in direct conflict with their psychosocial stage of development—the enjoyment of retirement, spousal re-establishment, self-reflection and life review (Walsh 2005).

Of the 2.7 million grandparents mentioned above, only 1.7 million were still in the labor force (US Census Bureau 2010). The remainder were likely to be relying on Social Security income or other types of public assistance. The financial burden of caring for grandchildren can be high. Not only do the household expenses increase, but also there are increased expenses for childcare, after-school activities and healthcare.

The health needs of grandparent(s) can also be a potential struggle for these families. For those grandparents with chronic health problems, increased caregiver burden can increase functional and cognitive impairment, type and amount of care, supervision needed and behavioral problems (Dowdell 2004; Chou 2000; Davidhizar *et al.* 2000; DesRoches *et al.* 2002; Grinstead *et al.* 2003). A United States study in 1997 found that 25.1 percent of grandparents raising grandchildren experienced depression, compared with 14.5 percent among non-caregiving grandparents (Minkler *et al.* 1997).

There is a double generation gap in grandfamilies, which can increase misunderstanding and conflict in the home. The greatest differences often relate to technology, music and social tolerance. Grandparents who pretend to be morally superior and see the younger generation as "going to the dogs" may alienate their grandchildren. Generational differences may also include how family conflicts are addressed, how education should be approached, etc.

Strengths

In terms of parenting, grandparents have already "been there and done that." They have had previous experiences in raising their own children, which may result in having more competent feelings toward childrearing. Harrison *et al.* (2000) found that grandparents who were caregivers for children with behavioral problems reported lower stress levels than both single and married parents with behaviorally disordered children.

Grandchildren can be a source of pleasure and provide companionship (Kropf and Burnette 2003). They may provide grandparents with opportunities for new activities and a renewed focus on life (Waldrop and Weber 2001). Research shows that many grandparents have voluntarily taken guardianship/custody of their grandchild/ren, conveying a desire to protect them from being placed outside of the family and a dedication to keeping their families intact (Harrison *et al.* 2000; Jendrek 1994). Because of this commitment, many of these grandparents have a sense of pride, self-respect and accomplishment (Dellman-Jenkins, Blankemeyer and Olesh 2002).

Grandparents can also be a link to family history for grandchildren. A grandchild living with grandparents can gain opportunities to participate in traditions that may not have been practiced with their parents. These family traditions can be wonderful ways to affirm family cultures and maintain attachments (Lowenstein 2010).

Empirical Support for Treatment

Research has identified training, education groups and various concrete supports as enhancing grandparents' skills as primary caretakers (Harrison *et al.* 2000). Support groups allow grandparents to feel less isolated and vent parenting frustration with their peers (Dellman-Jenkins *et al.* 2002). Respite care is important for stress management and may be particularly necessary for those grandparents with heath issues (Dolbin-MacNab 2006).

Roles change when grandparents become caregivers, which can lead to hierarchy difficulties between grandparents and grandchildren. Grandparents may have difficulty taking on disciplinary roles and children can develop inappropriate levels of power and control in the family (Hoshino 2008). Structural family therapy focuses on these kinds of family interactions and addresses boundary issues pertaining to these problems.

While not specific to grandparent families, there are several effective cognitive behavioral interventions/programs that address behavioral problems with children (i.e. The Incredible Years, Coping Power Program, Triple P—Positive Parenting Program, etc.). All of these include strong parent/caregiver components that emphasize limit-setting, impulse control, problem-solving and positive reinforcement (Lochman, Wells and Murray 2007; Reid and Webster-Stratton 2001; Sanders 2012).

Resources

- Grandparents.com—an online magazine: www.grandparents.com/family-and-relationships/caring-for-children

- Government information for grandparents raising grandchildren: www.usa.gov/Topics/Grandparents.shtml

- Grandparents Raising Grandchildren, Published by Child Welfare Information Gateway: https://www.childwelfare.gov/preventing/pdfs/grandparents.pdf

- AARP—information for grandparents raising their grandchildren: www.aarp.org/grandparents

- Grand Parent Again—support resources: www.grandparentagain.com

Counselor Cautions

Research identifies support groups as a helpful resource for grandparent-headed families (Longoria 2009; Kopera-Frye, Wiscott and Begovic 2003; Scannapieco 1999; Wohl, Lahner and Jooste 2003). If support groups are not available, counselors should be prepared to assist with finding other means of support. Therapists should be familiar with local resources in the area in order to link these families to necessary supports.

Counselors should be knowledgeable about their state and agency's policies regarding services provided by caregivers. It is likely that you will need to be prepared to verify the grandparents' guardianship to ensure that they do have legal rights to seek counseling for their grandchild. This can be difficult as some grandparents are left to care for their grandchildren without adequate notification and therefore are not likely to have the necessary documentation in order to request services for their grandchildren. It would also be helpful for counselors to be knowledgeable in resources in order to pursue legal guardianship and/or obtain written permission to provide services. There are situations where counselors must be prepared to deal with the child's biological parents as well, and/or assist the grandparent in how to deal with their own grown up child.

Counselors should be conscientious regarding the times they schedule appointments for grandparent families. Appointments should be made in the daytime, as grandparents may have trouble driving at night. Sessions should also be in areas where there is little to no background noise if hearing is problematic for grandparents.

Discussion Questions

- How did you end up living with your grandparent(s)? Was it sudden or did you know that you were going to be living there?

- Do you feel as if you can talk about your mother/father?

- Do you have any questions about why you are living with your grandparent(s)?
- What do you and your grandparent(s) have in common?
- What types of activities would make time together more fun?
- What are the obstacles to having more fun together? How could you overcome these?
- Do you ever worry about your grandmother/grandfather's health?
- What might be a fair way to help out around the house?

Ideas for Between-Session Homework

- Direct the family to create a chore chart to make the household duties easier to handle. Make sure you delegate age-appropriate chores and allow all members to have input in the creation of the chart.
- Encourage the family to do activities together—movie night, game night, meals together, visits to extended families, etc.
- Encourage the grandparents to participate in school meetings and other activities that their grandchildren are involved in and vice versa. For example, if it is age appropriate, allow the child to go to bingo night.
- Encourage the family to start/renew family traditions.
- Recommend that the grandparent(s) have a "parent's night out"—time for them to have some respite from parenting duties.
- If placement with grandparents is temporary or there is still biological parent involvement, assign the child the activity of creating a scrapbook of their favorite things, achievements, photos, special papers, etc. that they can share with their parent(s) during visits or when they go back to reside with their parent(s).

Therapeutic Activities

Activities included in this section are variations of evidenced-based practices tailored to be utilized with grandparent/kinship-headed families. Not all activities will apply to every family. Counselors should select those activities that best address a specific family's problem(s).

"WE ARE FAMILY" PARTY

PARTICIPANTS

Parent/caregiver(s) and children (all ages)

PURPOSE

To increase family cohesion, re-establish family traditions and increase nurturing

MATERIALS

- Large piece of paper or dry erase board or flip chart
- Construction paper
- Crayons/markers

DESCRIPTION

Discuss with the family the importance of family celebrations and how they provide feelings of togetherness and cohesion. Explain that birthdays are common celebrations shared by many families and that they will be planning a celebration of their family's "birthday." On a large piece of paper (or dry erase board or flip chart) write the following elements of a birthday party: Guests, Activities and Food. Ask the family to brainstorm what should be listed under each category.

- Guests—Who will be invited to the party? What is our limit? How many adults and how many children should there be? Who would appreciate this kind of celebration?
- Activities—What types of games would there be at the party? Would there be speeches or stories? What family traditions would be included? Would there be music?
- Refreshments—What types of food would be served? Are there any traditional or special family foods that should be served?

Then give each family member enough pieces of construction paper so that they can make cards for one another. Ask them to write very specific appreciation messages to one another in these cards and then have them give each other the cards at the end of the session.

DISCUSSION QUESTIONS

- When brainstorming ideas for your family "birthday" party, were there people who you didn't invite to the party? Why?
- Was there a game/activity that you would not be willing to play?
- Are there any family traditions that haven't been practiced for a while? Why? Would you like to start practicing them again?
- Do you have any ideas for "new" family traditions or celebrations?
- How did it feel to have family members say nice things about you in your cards?

RADIO SHOW

PARTICIPANTS

Grandparent/caregiver(s) and one child (ages 10–18)

PURPOSE

To improve communication

MATERIALS

- Sound recording device such as a Dictaphone or mobile phone
- Music

DESCRIPTION

Explain to grandparent/caregiver(s) that sometimes day-to-day responsibilities hinder families from really getting to know and enjoying each another. Explain that in this exercise one child will be interviewing and recording the grandparent/caregiver(s) as if they were guests on a radio talk show. Have the child come up with a name for her/his show, the music that s/he would like to play on the show and a list of questions to ask the grandparent/caregiver(s). Start recording, and get the child to introduce her/himself and the name of the show before conducting the interview. At the end of the show make sure that the child thanks the grandparents/caregiver(s) for being a guest.

DISCUSSION QUESTIONS

- *<To grandparent(s) only>* Were there any questions that surprised you or were hard to answer?
- *<To child only>* What answer(s) surprised you? How did that change the image that you have of your grandparent(s)?
- *<To grandparent(s) only>* How did it feel getting interviewed? What did you like or not like about it?
- *<To child only>* Were there answers that sparked your interest and created more questions? Do you have any additional questions for your grandparent(s) now?
- Would you recommend this activity to other grandfamilies? Why or why not?

GAINING PERSPECTIVE

PARTICIPANTS

Grandparent/caregiver(s) and children (ages 6–18)

PURPOSE

To increase communication and flexibility

MATERIALS

- List of statements (below)
- Two pieces of paper
- Marker

DESCRIPTION

Explain to family members that people often assume that others feel the same way they do and it is sometimes surprising to discover differences of opinion. Explain that in this activity everyone will be expressing a different opinion but they are simply to observe one another and *not* make comments. On one piece of paper make a large minus (–) sign and place it on one side of the room; on the other piece of paper make a large plus (+) sign and place it on the opposite side of the room. Explain that the space between the two signs represents a continuum (or scale) showing how much you agree or disagree. The end where the plus (+) sign is means "strongly agree," the end with the minus (–) sign means "strongly disagree" and the middle of the room means neither. Tell family members that you will be reading various statements and that after each one they should stand in the place that best represents their feelings. If necessary, give an example before beginning.

Examples of statements that can be used (but add relevant individualized statements):

- I'm feeling comfortable right now.
- I feel good about what the rules are at home.
- I get along with other family members.
- I have more good days than bad days.
- I feel like my family listens to me.
- I listen to my family without interrupting them.
- I feel hopeful about the future.
- There are things I worry about.

DISCUSSION QUESTIONS

- What did you notice about where you stood in relation to others? What were the similarities? What were the differences?
- What do you think the purpose of this activity was?
- Was it difficult not to make comments about where others placed themselves during the activity?
- Were you surprised about anyone's placement choice?
- Are there other statements that you would like to include to see where other family members place themselves?

HEALING OUR HEARTS

PARTICIPANTS

Grandparent/caregiver(s) and children (ages 6–18)

PURPOSE

To increase communication and to identify family strengths

MATERIALS

- Large poster board
- Pack of construction paper
- Scissors
- Glue sticks
- Crayons or markers

DESCRIPTION

Prior to the family's arrival, cut a large heart out of the large piece of poster board and hang it on a wall. Explain to family members that discussing painful experiences in our lives can be difficult but that having the support of family can help ease the pain. Ask everyone to choose three different colors of construction paper. Instruct them to cut a heart out of *one* of their pieces and to write on it what hurts them (i.e. things that cause them to feel sad, hurt, worried, scared etc.). Allow family members to share what they wrote on their hearts. Explain that the large heart represents their family, and instruct them to glue their individual hearts inside the larger family heart. Ask family members to trace their left hands and then their right hands (one hand on each of the remaining two pieces of paper in their possession) and cut them out. Instruct them to write on one of the hands three things they *need* from their family to heal their hurts and to write three things they can *give* to the family to help heal others' hurts on the other hand. Allow family members to share and then ask them to glue their hands onto the large heart.

DISCUSSION QUESTIONS

- What was it like to share your hurts with your family?
- Are there hurts that you wanted to share but didn't?
- How were your hurts similar? How were they different?
- How can you let family members know when you're hurting?
- How did it feel to hear what other family members are willing to do to help heal your hurts? Did any of their ideas surprise you?
- How did it feel to think of yourself as able to offer help? How will you know when you can actually do some of the things you listed?

ROYAL BOUNDARIES

PARTICIPANTS

Grandparent/caregiver(s) and children (all ages)

PURPOSE

Establishing parent–child boundaries and encouraging consistent rules

MATERIALS

* A template of a crown (or purchase enough toy crowns for each family member to have one)
* Paper
* Scissors
* Crayons or markers
* Decorative stickers

DESCRIPTION

Explain to the family that boundaries can become blurred, especially when roles change. A traditional grandparent role is very different from a parent role, which can make it hard for grandparents to enforce rules. Tell the family that you will be appointing them members of the Royal Family. You will then assign family members as follows: a King and a Queen (the grandparents/caregivers) and Prince(s) and/or Princess(es) (the children in the family). Provide each family member with a crown and instruct them to design their crown based upon their title in the royal family. Ask the family to identify behaviors of their royal status—what s/he would do as the King/Queen/Prince/ Princess. These may include things such as, a "good" King or Queen creates laws of the land and makes sure that the laws are followed, or a "good" Prince or Princess follows the laws of the King and Queen. The King and Queen should then outline the rules of the kingdom.

DISCUSSION QUESTIONS

* *<To grandchildren only>* What rules did the King or Queen set that you felt were inappropriate or unfair?
* *<To grandchildren only>* How do you feel you are treated by the King and Queen?
* Did the Prince(s) and Princess(es) listen to the King and Queen?
* What are the rules at home? Do they get followed?
* What is a benefit of following the rules? What are rules for? What would it be like not to have rules?
* *<To grandparent(s) only>* When are times that you can praise your grandchildren, even for the small things?

PHOTOSHOP

PARTICIPANTS
Children only (ages 5–18)

PURPOSE
To increase family cohesion and playfulness

MATERIALS
- Photocopies of old pictures of the grandparent(s)
- Paper
- Glue stick
- Pen, pencil or markers
- Small scrapbook or a ringbinder

DESCRIPTION
Prior to the session, ask grandparent/caregiver(s) to bring interesting/potentially humorous old photos of themselves to the session. Photocopy these pictures so as not to damage the original photos. Explain that there is a wide generation gap between grandparents and grandchildren and how humor can be a wonderful way to bridge the gap. Instruct the children to take the photocopies of their grandparents' photos and make a scrapbook of them with funny captions. The grandparent(s) can be brought in at the end of the session and grandchildren can share their humorous captions.

DISCUSSION QUESTIONS
- *<To grandchildren only>* What was it like to see the pictures of your grandparent(s)? Had you seen them before?
- *<To grandchildren only>* What did you notice about the pictures? Was there anything that interested you about a particular picture? Do you have any questions about the pictures?
- What made you pick the caption for each picture? Was it something spontaneous that you made up or was there a reason behind what you chose?
- *<To grandparent(s) only>* Were you able to laugh at the grandkids' captions?
- *<To grandparent(s) only>* What funny captions might you have used for some of the pictures?

FAMILY COLLAGE

PARTICIPANTS
Grandparent/caregiver(s) and children (ages 6–18)

PURPOSE
To increase family cohesion and appreciation

MATERIALS

- Shoebox with an opening in the top (large enough to slide a piece of paper in)
- Old magazines
- Scissors
- Glue stick

DESCRIPTION
Explain to the family that it can be difficult to remember to compliment one another as we go about busy lives. Tell the family that they will be creating a collage compliment box. Using magazines in order to find words and pictures that represent themselves as individuals and as a family, everyone should take turns gluing something new to the box until it is completely covered with pictures and words. Once completed, encourage the family to take it home and to use it to place written compliments/appreciations for one another in it. Suggest that the contents of the box can be read once a week at family dinners or the family can bring it to counseling sessions to be read there.

DISCUSSION QUESTIONS

- What was making the collage with your family like? Were you able to take turns and be respectful of one another's pictures?
- What do you like the best about the collage?
- Is there a picture or phrase that was added that you're curious about?
- Why is it important to remember positive things about each other? Why is it important to hear the positive things about yourself?
- When do you think it would be best to read the contents of the box?
- How can you keep this going? What are ways that you can make giving each other positive comments a part of your daily lives?

"PEACE" OF THE PIE

PARTICIPANTS
Grandparent/caregiver(s) only

PURPOSE
To recognize the need for and identify ways to increase self-care

MATERIALS

- White board or flip chart
- Dry erase markers
- Paper
- Pencil or pen
- Scissors
- Tape

DESCRIPTION
Explain to grandparent/caregiver(s) that life is full of commitments and responsibilities, and it can be difficult to find peace amongst the chaos. Provide the grandparent/caregiver(s) with a piece of paper, and ask them to list all the different things they spend time doing during the day (i.e., work, cooking, cleaning, watching television, running errands, children's sporting events/activities, hobbies, self-care, etc.). Ask them to draw a large circle or "pie" on the white board (or flip chart) representing all the hours in a day. Ask them to draw dividing lines, "cutting their pie" into appropriate-sized slices to represent how much time they spend on each of the commitments/activities they listed. Ask them to write the corresponding commitments/activities inside each piece of pie. Then explain that self-care is an essential part of stress management. Ask what they would like it to look like if they could change the sizes of the slices of the pie. Instruct them to draw another circle and repeat the exercise but this time dividing the "pie" the way that they would *like* it to be.

DISCUSSION QUESTIONS

- How were your two "pies" different?

- What are the most important pieces of your "pie"?

- Have there been other times in your life when you were better at self-care? What were those times like for you?

- How can you increase your self-care time? What kinds of things do you like to do for self-care? Are there any that you didn't list?

- Looking at the first and second "pies," how can you accomplish those changes? What ideas do you have for making more time for the things that you would like to do? Would this include respite care (where someone else takes the children for an evening or a day or a weekend)?

GUESS WHO?

PARTICIPANTS

Grandparent/caregiver(s) and children (ages 8–18)*
* There must be more than two people for this activity

PURPOSE

To increase family cohesion, communication and acceptance

MATERIALS

- Index cards
- Paper
- Pen or pencils

DESCRIPTION

Explain that large generation gaps can sometimes cause family members to be judgmental of one another. Provide each family member with three index cards and ask them to write down their responses to each one of the following on different index cards.

1. A personal accomplishment (something you are proud of).
2. Something you believe in (a value).
3. A personal goal (what you are working on to make yourself a better person—i.e. patience, self-control, tenacity, etc.).

Ask family members *not* to look at what others have written. Then collect all of the cards and mix them up. Read each card out loud one at a time and have family members write down on a piece of paper who they believe wrote that particular card. When everyone has written down their answers, ask the person whose response it was to speak up. Ask who guessed correctly. Then repeat until all of the cards have been read.

DISCUSSION QUESTIONS

- What factors or traits did you consider when making your guesses?
- Did any of the cards surprise you? Why? Did you make any prejudicial assumptions about anyone?
- What did you learn about your family members?
- Were there any huge differences in goals or values? How do you think those differences affect your relationships? How do you accept other people's beliefs when they are different from your own?

- Were there any similarities in your responses? What do you think this means?

- How can you use your similarities to improve your interactions at home, school, work, etc.?

FAMILY TREE

PARTICIPANTS

Grandparent/caregiver(s) and children (ages 6–18)

PURPOSE

To increase family cohesion and to identify family strengths

MATERIALS

- Photocopies of pictures of family members

- Poster board

- Crayons or markers

- Tape or glue stick

DESCRIPTION

Prior to the session, ask the grandparent/caregiver(s) to bring pictures of as many family members as possible. Make photocopies of these in order to prevent damage to the original pictures. Discuss with family members the large combination of factors that make individuals who they are. Explain that one of those factors is ancestors. Instruct the family to use the photocopies to create a "family tree" on the poster board in whatever way they would like. If there are family members whose pictures are not available, the family can draw the person or simply write their name(s) where s/he belongs. After everyone has been placed in the family tree, ask family members to share what they know about each person, paying particular attention to each family member's personal strengths.

DISCUSSION QUESTIONS

- What was making a family tree like for you? Were there happy parts in creating it? Sad parts?

- Were you surprised by anything?

- Is there anyone that was purposely left out? Why?

- Are there family members that you would like to know more about?

- Are there family members that you would like to visit?

- Which family member do you relate to the most?

- Which family members are you most like?

Additional Activities That May be Helpful

- Mother May I? in Chapter 3: Single-Parent Families with an Absent Parent (p.25)

- Boundary Pies in Chapter 3: Single-Parent Families with an Absent Parent (p.31)

- Giving Choices in Chapter 7: Families with an Incarcerated Loved One (p.99)

- Round Robin "I" Statements in Chapter 8: Families with a Substance-Abusing Child (p.114)

- Parenting Consistency in Chapter 9: Families with Parent Substance Abuse (p.129)

- A Bag of Coping in Chapter 10: Families with a Mentally Ill Parent (p.148)

- Rocking with Peace Chapter 11: Families with a Chronically Ill Child (p.163)

References

Burnette, D. (1997) "Grandparents raising grandchildren in the inner city." *Families in Society,* September, 489–499.

Caliandro, G. and Hughes, C. (1998) "The experience of being a grandmother who is the primary caregiver for her HIV-positive grandchild." *Nursing Research 47,* 2, 107–113.

Chou, K.R. (2000) "Caregiver burden: a concept analysis." *Journal of Pediatric Nursing 15,* 6, 398–407.

Davidhizer, R., Bechtel, G.A. and Woodring, B.C. (2000) "The changing role of grandparenthood." *Journal of Gerontological Nursing 26,* 1, 24–29.

Dellman-Jenkins, M., Blankemeyer, M. and Olesh, M. (2002) "Adults in extended grandparent roles: considerations for practice, policy and research." *Educational Gerontology 28,* 219–235.

DesRoches, C., Blendon, R., Grinstead, L.N., Young, J., Scoles, K. and Kim, M. (2002) "Caregiving in the post-hospitalization period: findings from a national survey." *Nursing Economics 20,* 5, 216–224.

Dolbin-MacNab, M.L. (2006) "Just like raising your own? Grandmothers' perceptions of parenting a second time around." *Family Relations 55,* 564–575.

Dowdell, E.B. (2004) "Grandmother caregivers and caregiver burden." *Medical Consultants Network 29,* 5, 300–304.

Dressel, P.L. and Barnhill, S.K. (1994) "Reframing gerontological thought and practice: the case of grandmothers with daughters in prison." *The Gerontologist 34,* 5, 585–591.

Fuller-Thomson, E. and Minkler, M. (2000) "African American grandparents raising grandchildren: a national profile of demographic and health characteristics." *Health Social Work 25,* 2, 109–118.

Goodman, C. and Silverstein, M. (2002) "Grandmothers raising grandchildren: family structure and well-being in culturally diverse families." *The Gerotologist 42,* 5, 676–689.

Grant, R. (2000) "The special needs of children in kinship care." *Journal of Gerontological Social Work 33,* 17–33.

Grinstead, L.N., Leder, S., Jensen, S. and Bond, L. (2003) "Review of research on health of caregiving grandparents." *Journal of Advanced Nursing 44,* 3, 318–326.

Harrison, K.A., Richman, G.L. and Vittimberga, G.L. (2000) "Parental stress in grandparents versus parents raising children with behavior problems." *Journal of Family Issues 21,* 2, 262–270.

Hoshino, J. (2008) "Structural Family Art Therapy." In C. Kerr, J. Hoshino, J. Sutherland, S.T. Parashak and L.L. McCarley (eds) *Family Art Therapy: Foundations of Theory and Practice.* New York: Routledge.

Jendrek, M.P. (1994) "Grandparents who parent their grandchildren: circumstances and decisions." *The Gerontologist 34*, 206–216.

Joslin, D. and Brouard, A. (1995) "The prevalence of grandmothers as primary caregivers in a poor pediatric population." *The Journal of Community Health 20*, 5, 383–401.

Kopera-Frye, K., Wiscott, R.C. and Begovic, A. (2003) "Lessons Learned from Custodial Grandparents Involved in a Community Support Group." In B. Hayslip and J.H. Patrick (eds) *Working with Custodial Grandparents*. New York: Springer Publishing.

Kropf, N.P. and Burnette, D. (2003) "Grandparents as family caregivers: lessons for intergenerational education." *Educational Gerontology 29*, 361–372.

Lochman, J. E., Wells, K. C. and Murray, M. (2007) "The Coping Power Program: Preventive Intervention at the Middle School Transition." In P. Tolan, J. Szapocznik and S. Sambrano (eds) *Preventing Youth Substance Abuse: Science-Based Programs for Children and Adolescents*. Washington, DC: American Psychological Association.

Longoria, R.A. (2009) "Grandparents raising grandchildren: perceived neighborhood risk as a predictor of emotional well-being." *Journal of Human Behavior in the Social Environment 19*, 483–511.

Lowenstein, L. (2010) *Creative Family Therapy Techniques: Play, Art, and Expressive Activities to Engage Children in Family Sessions*. Toronto, Ontario: Champion Press.

Minkler, M., Fuller-Thomson, E., Miller, D. and Driver, D. (1997) "Depression in grandparents raising grandchildren: results of a national longitudinal study." *Archives of Family Medicine 6*, 5, 445–52.

Minkler, M. and Roe, K.M. (1993) *Grandmothers as Caregivers: Raising Children of the Crack Cocaine Epidemic*. Newbury Park, CA: Sage.

Mutchler, J.E., Lee, S. and Baker, L.A. (2003) *Grandparent Care in the African-American Population*. Boston: Gerontology Institute, University of Massachusetts.

Reid, M. J. and Webster-Stratton, C. (2001) "The Incredible Years—parent, teacher, and child intervention: targeting multiple areas of risk for a young child with pervasive conduct problems using a flexible, manualized, treatment program." *Journal of Cognitive and Behavior Practice 8*, 377–386.

Sanders, M.R. (2012) "Development, evaluation, and multinational dissemination of the Triple P-Positive Parenting Program." *Annual Review of Clinical Psychology 8*, 345–379.

Scannapieco, M. (1999) "Formal Kinship Care Practice Models." In R.L. Hegar and M. Scannapierco (eds) *Kinship Foster Care: Policy, Practice, and Research*. New York: Oxford University Press.

US Census Bureau (2008) *American Community Survey*. Suitland, MD: US Census Bureau. Available at www.census.gov/acs/www/data_documentation/2008_release, accessed 4 December 2013.

US Census Bureau (2010) *American Community Survey*. Suitland, MD: US Census Bureau. Available at www.census.gov/acs/www/data_documentation/2010_release, accessed 4 December 2013.

Waldrop, D.P and Weber, J.A (2001) "From grandparent to caregiver: the stress and satisfaction of raising grandchildren." *Families in Society 82*, 461–472.

Walsh, F. (2005) "Families in Later Life: Challenges and Opportunities." In B. Carter and M. McGoldrick (eds) *The Expanded Family Life Cycle: Individual, Family and Social Perspectives*. New York: Pearson.

Wohl, E.C., Lahner, J.M. and Jooste, J. (2003) "Group Processes Among Grandparents Raising Grandchildren." In B. Hayslip and J.H. Patrick (eds) *Working with Custodial Grandparents*. New York: Springer Publishing.

CHAPTER 7

Families with an Incarcerated Loved One

Introduction

More parents than ever are being incarcerated. The United States has the highest imprisonment rate in the world (Pew Charitable Trusts 2008). Half of those imprisoned in the United States are parents of children under the age of 18 (Glaze and Maruschak 2008; Walmsley 2009). A quarter of African American children born in the United States in 1990 experienced parental incarceration by their 14th birthday (Wildeman 2009). Most children born in the United States with an incarcerated parent had a father in prison (91 percent), but increasing numbers of children have a mother in prison—the number of incarcerated mothers doubled between 1991 and 2007 (Murray, Farrington and Sekol 2012).

Of the incarcerated parents in the United States, 61 percent of mothers and 42 percent of fathers were living with at least one of their children at the time of incarceration and 50 percent of imprisoned mothers and fathers provided primary financial support for their children before incarceration (Glaze and Maruschak 2008). When children did not reside with a parent, they lived with grandparents, other relatives, foster families and friends or others (Murray, Farrington and Sekol 2012).

Families experiencing incarceration have varied contexts including:

- whether the father or mother is the incarcerated parent
- the quality of parent–child relationships prior to incarceration
- the offense for which the parent was incarcerated and the length of sentence
- how recent the incarceration was
- contact with the incarcerated parent
- how individual family members cope with the incarceration
- levels of social support

- economic resources

- parental substance abuse or mental illness

- care arrangements during parental incarceration (Johnson and Waldfogel 2004; Murray and Farrington 2008; Parke and Clarke-Stewart 2003).

Potential Challenges/Vulnerabilities

Incarceration creates many challenges for families of prisoners. One difficult area is the shame and social stigma that they feel (Braman 2004; Condry 2007). This can often lead to isolation, secrecy and "hiding" behaviors (Nesmith and Ruhland 2008). Research suggests that shame is associated with chronic anger, depression, expressions of hostility and relationship difficulties (Tangney and Dearing 2002).

The shame surrounding the parent's crime means that children are often not given honest explanations about the whereabouts of their incarcerated parent. It is estimated that approximately one third of children are told lies, one third are told an altered version of the truth and one third are told the entire truth (Council on Crime and Justice 2006).

Caregivers and partners also face stigma. They report feeling criticized by others for becoming involved with someone who is incarcerated and report that people make false assumptions about their own values and behaviors (Council on Crime and Justice 2006).

Research also shows that children of incarcerated parents are more likely than other children to be arrested themselves (Murray and Farrington 2005). Parental incarceration is associated with higher risk for children's externalizing and antisocial behavior, although this phenomenon may be attributed to more family conflict, more problems with family cohesion and less family structure—the byproducts of incarceration (Aaron and Dallaire 2010).

Parental incarceration can also reduce quality of caregiving to children. Caregivers struggle to find balance between their own coping and helping their children (Council on Crime and Justice 2006). They are stressed from financial problems, the sole care of children and supporting an incarcerated partner (Richards *et al.* 1994). These stressors can lead to decreased supervision and attention to children (Bocknek, Sanderson and Britner 2009; Murray 2005).

Finally, families often lack dependable contacts with their incarcerated loved one. Factors such as distance/cost of travel, conflicted family relationships and inconvenient visiting times make it difficult for families to visit (Murray 2007). Telephone communication is limited because of the cost of calls from prison (Braman 2004). In addition, caregivers often become gatekeepers for children's visits. Many former spouses or partners are reluctant to maintain relationships, particularly if the incarcerated family member had been violent. In some cases, it may be in the family's best interests to limit contact.

Strengths

Despite evidence that children of incarcerated parents are at higher risk of antisocial behaviors, many children do not misbehave. Among those resilient children, there appears to be *better* family relationships and cohesion while their parent was incarcerated (Poehlmann *et al.* 2008).

Families of incarcerated loved ones do find ways to get support. Church and faith appear to be particularly important. Church offers a support group, while faith provides an explanation for life's struggles and promises that suffering is not all for nothing. Extended family connections also provide vital support, and many children of incarcerated parents find places outside of the home to boost their self-esteem. Most of these include sports, drama, church or finding a close friend (Council on Crime and Justice 2006).

Empirical Support for Potential Treatment Approaches

Children who regularly visit their parent demonstrate better emotional and social adjustment, as well as a lower degree of juvenile delinquency. Teens who have more frequent contact with incarcerated mothers experience less school dropout and fewer suspensions than those teens with less contact (Trice and Brewster 2004). Incarcerated fathers involved in an enhanced visitation program with their children reported enhanced relationships and communication with their children, increased family cohesion and improved child behavior (Dunn and Arbuckle 2002). However, it is important for counselors to determine the type and quality of relationships on a case-by-case basis. Not all incarcerated parents serve as an attachment figure for their child(ren).

Nesmith and Ruhland (2008) found that children who had incarcerated parents and were involved in extracurricular activities showed a higher degree of resilience. Extracurricular activities have been shown in the general population to improve grades and school attendance, improve self-esteem and decrease misbehavior (Mahoney and Cairns 1997; Marsh 1992).

Marin, Bohanek and Fivush (2008) found that families who were open and honest about discussing difficult topics showed improved social and academic outcomes. Nesmith and Ruhland (2008) suggested that children be given developmentally appropriate information regarding their incarcerated parents, as children form their own erroneous conclusions about what has happened or what will happen in the future if they are not given accurate information.

Mackintosh *et al.* (2006) found that children of incarcerated mothers had fewer problem behaviors when they felt more warmth and acceptance from *caregivers.* This suggests that caregiving interventions may be as helpful to children of incarcerated parents as interventions that focus exclusively on the child–incarcerated-parent relationship.

Resources

- *Family Members Behind Bars: Difficult Questions Children Ask... and Answers that Might Help* (published by Montana Alliance of Families Touched by Incarceration (MAFTI)): www.f2f.ca.gov/res/pdf/FamilyMembersBehindBars.pdf

- *How to Explain...Jails and Prisons...to Children: A Caregiver's Guide* (published by California Department of Corrections and Rehabilitation): www.f2f.ca.gov/res/pdf/HowToExplainJails.pdf

- *What Do Children of Prisoners and their Caregivers Need?* (published by the Children of Prisoners Library: www.f2f.ca.gov/res/pdf/WhatDoChildren.pdf

- National Resource Center hosted by Family and Corrections Network: http://fcnetwork.org

- Prison Activist Resource Center: www.prisonactivist.org/resources

Counselor Cautions

Counselors should examine their own attitudes, experiences and biases related to law-breaking behavior and incarceration. It is important for counselors to maintain objectivity regarding the incarcerated parent, because judgmental attitudes only perpetuate the family's shame. This can significantly interfere with the therapeutic relationship.

On the other side, partners and children of incarcerated parents may have a difficult time trusting systems that have separated them from their loved one. They may see counseling as one of those systems. Counselors should take extra time and make extra efforts to engage and join with the family.

If the counselor has more information about the incarcerated parent than the children know, it is important for the counselor to refrain from disclosing this information. It is the family's responsibility to share information. Counselors can facilitate this discussion between parent/caregiver(s) and children (and they can certainly share with the parent/caregiver(s) the benefits of dispelling confusion) but they should not be the ones to disclose information.

While counselors may be more comfortable with the psychological/emotional/interactional aspects of helping, families with incarcerated loved ones often need concrete assistance. It is important for counselors to become familiar with resources in their communities so that they can make appropriate referrals for housing, respite care, support groups, etc.

Discussion Questions

- What are your family's strengths?

- What types of activities do you enjoy doing together? What would you *like* to do together?

- Do you get to visit or communicate with your incarcerated loved one? How does it go? How do you come back feeling?

- Does your family openly talk about your loved one being incarcerated? Do you understand what happened?

- How do family members handle their frustrated and angry feelings? Does this feel safe?

- How has family life changed since your loved one became incarcerated?

- What needs does your family have at this time?

Ideas for Between-Session Homework

- Encourage caregivers to spend additional quality time with children. Recommend activities such as family meals, reading to younger children, games nights, etc.

- Direct caregivers to work with children in finding appropriate extracurricular activities to become involved in. Examples include student government, band, church youth groups, sports teams, chess clubs, debate teams, dance teams, drama performance groups, etc.

- Encourage caregivers to sign children up for mentoring programs that their schools might provide

- Teach caregivers to keep track of children's positive behaviors and to bring these to sessions. Then facilitate discussions about the *meanings* of these positive behaviors. For example, you may ask, "What do you think this says about you as a person?"

- Encourage caregivers to contact children's teachers and to schedule conferences in order to form better school–home connections.

- If younger children are visiting the incarcerated parent, send several children's books and a recording device so that the parent can record her/his voice reading the stories. Suggest that children listen to this whenever they wish to hear their parent's voice.

Therapeutic Activities

Activities included in this section are experiential opportunities to address typical but specific family issues related to parent incarceration. Not all activities will apply to every family. Counselors should select those activities that best address a specific family's problem(s).

THE WEIGHT OF SHAMEFUL THOUGHTS

PARTICIPANTS
Parent/caregiver(s) and children (ages 7–18)

PURPOSE
To reduce shame

MATERIALS
- Backpacks or bags
- Rocks or bricks
- Paper
- Pen or pencil
- Tape

DESCRIPTION
Prior to the family's arrival, locate enough backpacks or bags so that each family member can have one. Fill each of the backpacks/bags with heavy rocks or bricks with shameful and negative self-statements written on paper and taped to them. Shameful self-statements can be similar to the following.

- The kids at school hate me.
- Everyone thinks I'm bad because my mom/dad went to jail.
- It's my fault that my mom/dad went to jail.
- No one would like me if they knew about my family.
- It's so embarrassing to tell kids where my mom/dad is.

Ask all the family members to wear or carry their backpacks/bags and to walk around the room for a few minutes. When it becomes clear that family members are becoming tired from the weight of the backpacks/bags tell them to stop. Explain that the backpack is full of shameful self-talk, and it is time to get rid of the shame. Have family members take turns removing the rocks/bricks from their backpacks while reading each "thought" and then stating why it is inaccurate. After all the "shame rocks/bricks" have been removed from the backpacks, have family members wear/carry their empty backpacks/bags and walk around the room again. Then sit down for a follow-up discussion.

DISCUSSION QUESTIONS
- How difficult was it to carry around the bricks/rocks?
- Did it get easier or harder as you walked around a bit? How is that like shame?
- Which of the shameful statements was closest to what you think sometimes?

- What was it like to get rid of the "shame" bricks/rocks?

- How can you get rid of your own shaming thoughts?

- How can you help each other get rid of shaming thoughts?

THE FEELINGS GAME

PLAYERS
Parent/caregiver(s) and children (ages 8–18)

PURPOSE
To express/reconcile feelings, reduce shame and increase empathy

MATERIALS

- Index cards

- Pen or pencil

DESCRIPTION
Prior to the family's arrival, using the feeling words listed below (and any other feelings that you think might be applicable), write down each feeling on enough index cards so that each family member will have one of *each* feeling (i.e. if you have four family members you will need four "Hurt" cards, etc.) When the family arrives, hand them each a stack of feelings cards and ask them to sort through their cards and select the three cards that best describe their feelings about their parent/loved one being incarcerated. When everyone has selected their three cards, go around the room and have family members guess what each other's three feelings are.

Suggested feelings words:

- hurt

- confused

- angry

- scared

- lost

- embarrassed

- sad

- lonely

- worried

- ashamed

- disappointed

- annoyed.

DISCUSSION QUESTIONS

- How well were you able to guess each other's feelings?

- Have you ever talked with anyone about these feelings?

- How hard is it for you to talk about these feelings as a family?

- Which feeling is the most uncomfortable for you?

- What do you do to comfort yourself when you have strong uncomfortable feelings?

- What do you need to do as a family to make talking about feelings more natural?

THE INTERVIEW

PARTICIPANTS
Parent/caregiver(s) and children (ages 5–18)

PURPOSE
To decrease confusion and inaccurate assumptions

MATERIALS

- Pretend microphones

- Notebooks (optional)

- Pens/pencils (optional)

DESCRIPTION
Explain to the family that, because of shame and worry, families often do not talk about the circumstances around their loved one's incarceration. This leads to confusion and inaccurate assumptions. Explain that in this exercise the children will pretend to be "reporters" at a "briefing" or "interview" and the caregiver(s) will be the "expert" who is being interviewed. Hand each child a "microphone" and a notepad with a pen or pencil. Encourage children to ask whatever questions they have about their parent's incarceration. Encourage everyone to do this in a somewhat playful manner, for example, holding the "microphones" up to their own mouths when asking a question, tilting the "microphones" towards the caregiver during her/his response and pretending to take notes in the notepad.

DISCUSSION QUESTIONS

- Did you get all of your questions answered? If not, do you need to ask anything now? Or is there somewhere you need to go to get that information?

- Is it helpful to understand more about your loved one's incarceration? How do you feel right now?

- Were you surprised by any of the information that you heard?

- *<To caregiver only>* Are you okay after being put on the spot? How difficult was it for you to answer all these questions?

- Is there any information that was given today that you do not want shared with any particular other persons?

- How well were you and the child/ren able to take turns in asking questions?

SUPPORT

PARTICIPANTS
Parent/caregiver(s) only

PURPOSE
To increase formal and informal caregiver support

MATERIALS

- Paper
- Pens/pencils

DESCRIPTION
Explain to the caregiver(s) that, like the children they are raising, caregivers are also affected by social stigma and shame. Because of this, they often do not share their situation with others, thereby limiting both formal and informal supports. Explain how important building a support network is. Then read the following list of potential Areas of Needed Support and ask the caregiver(s) to identify the three areas that support is most needed.

1. Financial
2. Emotional/mental health
3. Respite care
4. Transportation
5. Parenting—social/emotional/behavioral
6. Parenting—information regarding children of incarcerated parents

Then take out three sheets of paper. Write one of the three Areas of Needed Support at the top of each sheet of paper and make two columns underneath: one for "People" and one for "Agencies." Using one Area of Needed Support at a time, brainstorm with the caregiver(s) people and agencies that could assist with the identified support needs. Have the caregiver write these down. Be sure that you are familiar with your community's resources.

DISCUSSION QUESTIONS

- How comfortable are you asking for help/support when you need it?

- What are the barriers that prevent you from asking for support?

- What do you need to tell yourself so that you can feel more comfortable asking for help/support?

- Do you think that other people ask for help/support? How do you think they do it?

- Which area of support do you think you'll seek out first?

FAMILY TRADITIONS

PARTICIPANTS
Parent/caregiver(s) and children (ages 7–18)

PURPOSE
To enhance family cohesion

MATERIALS

- Dry erase board or chalk board

- Marker or chalk

DESCRIPTION
PART 1

Explain to the family what family traditions are (practices, customs or rituals that happen at regular intervals) such as birthday cakes, baptisms, bedtime stories etc. Then ask family members to brainstorm the various traditions that are in their family. Write these on the board so that everyone can see them.

DISCUSSION QUESTIONS

- How long have these traditions been in your family?

- Where did they come from?

- Who makes them happen?

- Which of these traditions are your favorites?

- Which are your least favorites?

- Are there any that you would like to change?

PART 2

Now ask the family to brainstorm ideas for new traditions that they might like to start in their family. Here are some examples.

- Birthday person gets to pick the dinner menu.

- Everyone says, "I love you" before going to bed.

- Everyone describes a success that they had that day at the dinner table.

- A special breakfast on Monday mornings.

- A once a month movie night.

Write these on the board so everyone can see them. Then ask the family which one(s) they would like to start doing.

COMPLIMENT HOT SEAT

PARTICIPANTS
Parent/caregiver(s) and children (ages 5–18)

PURPOSE
To enhance family cohesion and warmth

MATERIALS

- Chair

DESCRIPTION
Place a chair in the middle of the room and explain that this will be the "Hot Seat" and whoever is sitting in it will be receiving compliments from the other members in the family. Share the rules regarding compliments.

1. The compliment must be truthful and kind.

2. The compliment must not be about personal appearances or clothes.

3. No silly faces or voices.

Then ask the youngest member of the family to sit in the Hot Seat and instruct the remaining family members to each give her/him a compliment. Continue with the next youngest child until all family members have had an opportunity to sit in the Hot Seat.

DISCUSSION QUESTIONS

- What was it like to receive so many compliments from your family? What did you like about it or not like about it?

- What did you like and not like about *giving* compliments?

- Who had the easiest time accepting compliments graciously?

- Who had the hardest time accepting compliments graciously?

- When was the last time someone in the family gave a compliment prior to this activity?

- Who typically gives most of the compliments in your family?

- What do you think about giving compliments in day-to-day life?

- What stops you from giving more compliments?

REFLECTING, REFLECTING, REFLECTING

PARTICIPANTS

Parent/caregiver(s) and one child (ages 7–18)
*This is an activity for two people (rather than the entire family) but it can be repeated several times – one at a time with different children

PURPOSE

To enhance parent empathy, understanding and nurturing

MATERIALS

- None

DESCRIPTION

Explain that sometimes parents/caregivers get so busy taking care of the physical aspects of running a family that is difficult to find time to talk about feelings. Direct the caregiver and child to face one another. Using the topics below (or others that might seem appropriate) ask the child to take one to two minutes to describe them to the parent/caregiver one at a time. After s/he describes each one, instruct the parent/caregiver to respond with a reflective statement about the child's feelings or point of view. Do *not* let the parent add any other comments or explanations—only simple reflective statements that begin with the word, "You." (Note: A reflective statement is a statement that offers back to the speaker what the listener believes was conveyed.) Ask the child to tell the caregiver whether this is accurate and if it is *not* accurate, to share a more accurate description of her/his thoughts and feelings. Continue to the next topic until complete.

- Talk about a fun break time or lunchtime at school.

- Talk about a difficult break time or lunchtime at school.

- Talk about your teacher (or the last teacher that you had).

- Describe cleaning your room.

- Describe how you found out about your parent going to jail.

- Describe your family life over the last month.

DISCUSSION QUESTIONS

- What was this activity like for both of you?

- *<To caregiver only>* How difficult was it to work out the child's thoughts and feelings?

- *<To child only>* How did it feel when your caregiver was correct about your thoughts and feelings? What about when they were incorrect about your thoughts and feelings?

- What do you think was helpful about this activity?

- How do you think understanding one another's point of view would help when there is conflict?

- Are there any parts of this activity that you could use in day-to-day life?

FAMILY STRUCTURE

PARTICIPANTS
Parent/caregiver(s) and children (ages 7–18)

PURPOSE
To enhance family structure and increase rule-following

MATERIALS

- Dry erase board, chalk board or flip chart paper

- Marker or chalk

DESCRIPTION
Explain that family structure is very important for everyone's safety and for getting along, and that rules and consequences help to prepare children for living in the community as adults. While no one likes rules, learning to comply and handling the accompanying frustration are important life lessons. Draw two vertical parallel lines down the board/paper so that it is divided into three sections. Title the left section "Rules," the middle section "Consequences," and the right section "Rewards." Ask the parent/caregiver(s) to name some family rules and write these under "Rules" (i.e. no hitting, carry your plate from the table to the sink, do homework, etc.). Ask the children if there should be any other rules added to the list. If the parent/caregiver agrees to these, add them to the list. Then facilitate a discussion about the kinds of consequences and rewards that should follow compliance or noncompliance with these rules. Make sure that the consequences and rewards fit with the rule.

DISCUSSION QUESTIONS

- Why do families have rules?

- Do adults have rules that they have to follow (i.e. laws, policies, etc.)?

- What happens when adults don't follow rules?

- Which of your family rules are you glad about?

- Which of your family rules is hardest to follow? What would help you to follow it better?

ON THE LINE WITH FAIR FIGHTING RULES

PARTICIPANTS
Parent/caregiver(s) and children (ages 7–18)

PURPOSE
To improve self-awareness and conflict resolution skills

MATERIALS

- Masking tape

- Pen or pencil

DESCRIPTION
Place an 8–10 inch piece of masking tape in a straight line down the middle of the room. Write "Very true of me" at one end of it and "Not true of me at all" at the other end of it. Then explain to the family that all families have conflict—conflict is to be expected when people live together. What is important is to find ways to resolve it productively. Then tell the family that you will be reading several Fair Fighting Rules and you would like them to place themselves along the line based on how true the statement is of their fighting behavior. Read each of the following one at a time. When the family members have positioned themselves after each one, ask everyone if they agree with each other's placements. Then go on to the next one and continue until the list is complete.

- Remain calm.

- No blaming.

- Listen to the other person.

- Avoid name calling.

- Avoid negative body language (i.e. facial expressions, eye rolling, etc.).

- Be specific about what is bothering you.

- Avoid "hitting below the belt."

- Talk about one problem at a time.

DISCUSSION QUESTIONS

- Did you find yourselves mostly at the "Very true of me" end or the "Not true of me at all" end of the line?

- Were you fairly accurate in your perceptions of your fair fighting behaviors or did your family disagree with your positions frequently?

- Which of the Fair Fighting Rules does your family do a good job of? Which do you need to work on?

- Which of the Fair Fighting Rules would you like to see in your family?

- How can you help each other stick to your Fair Fighting Rules?

GIVING CHOICES

PARTICIPANTS
Parent/caregiver(s) only

PURPOSE
To reduce parent/caregiver–child conflict and to improve parenting

MATERIALS

- Appendix D
- Scissors

DESCRIPTION
Prior to the session, cut out the cards in Appendix D and place them face down on a table. When the parent/caregiver arrives, explain that it is often easier to get cooperation from children when they don't feel like their freedoms are being taken away. Giving children choices within limits is a good parenting technique and one that can increase compliance. Examples include wanting a child to:

- take medicine (i.e. a parent/caregiver might say, "Would you like to take your medicine with juice or water?")

- wear warm clothing (i.e. a parent/caregiver might say, "Would you like to wear your coat or your heavy sweater?")

- pick up toys (i.e. a parent/caregiver might say, "Do you want to pick up your toys with this basket or one by one?").

Then explain that you and the parent/caregiver(s) will take turns (yes, include yourself as a role model) turning over the cards, reading the parent wish on the card and coming up with a choice that could be given to the child in order to improve compliance.

DISCUSSION QUESTIONS

- How difficult overall was it for you to come up with ideas for choices?

- Did it get easier as you answered more cards?

- What could you do if your child refused both choices?

- How difficult do you think this will be to implement in your home?

- Sometimes it's hard to remember to give choices when you're upset—how can you calm yourself?

- Do you see any other barriers to implementing this at home? How could you overcome them?

Additional Activities That May be Helpful

- Guilt Gobblers in Chapter 3: Single-Parent Families with an Absent Parent (p.29)

- Dear Mom and/or Dad in Chapter 4: Divorced/Separated/Unmarried Families—Both parents available (p.47)

- "Peace" of the Pie in Chapter 6: Families with Grandparents as Caregivers (p.80)

- Underneath Angry Feelings in Chapter 8: Families with a Substance-Abusing Child (p.113)

- Round Robin "I" Statements in Chapter 8: Families with a Substance-Abusing Child (p.114)

- My Worry Box in Chapter 10: Families with a Mentally Ill Parent (p.146)

- A Bag of Coping in Chapter 10: Families with a Mentally Ill Parent (p.148)

- No More Stinkin' Thinkin' in Chapter 11: Families with a Chronically Ill Child (p.156)

References

Aaron, L. and Dallaire, D.H. (2010) "Parental incarceration and multiple risk experiences: effects on family dynamics and children's delinquency." *Journal of Youth and Adolescence 39*, 1471–1484.

Bocknek E., Sanderson J. and Britner P. (2009) "Ambiguous loss and posttraumatic stress in school-age children of prisoners." *Journal of Child and Family Studies 18*, 323–333.

Braman, D. (2004) *Doing Time on the Outside: Incarceration and Family Life in Urban America*. Ann Arbor, MI: University of Michigan Press.

Condry, R. (2007) *Families Shamed: The Consequences of Crime for Relatives of SERIOUS offenders*. Collumpton: Willan.

Council on Crime and Justice (2006) *Children of Incarcerated Parents*. Minneapolis, MN: Council on Crime and Justice. Available at www.crimeandjustice.org/researchReports/CCJ%20CIP%20FINAL%20 REPORT%20updated%201.30.08.pdf, accessed 5 December 2013.

Dunn, E. and Arbuckle, J.G. (2002) *Children of Incarcerated Parents and Enhanced Visitation Programs: Impacts of the Living Interactive Family Education (LIFE) Program*. Available at http://extension.missouri. edu/4hlife/documents/guide/4HLIFE_guide_appendix_09.pdf, accessed 14 February 2014.

Glaze, L.E. and Maruschak, L.M. (2008) *Bureau of Justice Statistics Special Report: Parents in Prison and their Minor Children*. Washington, DC: Bureau of Justice Statistics.

Johnson, E.I. and Waldfogel, J. (2004) "Children of Incarcerated Parents: Multiple Risks and Children's Living Arrangements." In M. Pattillo, D. Weiman and B. Western (eds) *Imprisoning America: The Social Effects of Mass Incarceration*. New York: Russell Sage Foundation.

Mackintosh, V.H., Myers, B.J. and Kennon, S.S. (2006) "Children of incarcerated mothers and their caregivers: factors affecting the quality of their relationship." *Journal of Child and Family Studies 15*, 581–596.

Mahoney, J. and Cairns, R. (1997) "Do extracurricular activities protect against early school dropout?" *Developmental Psychology 33*, 241–253.

Marin, K.A., Bohanek, J.G. and Fivush, R. (2008) "Positive effects of talking about the negative: family narratives of negative experiences and preadolescents' perceived competence." *Journal of Research on Adolescence 18*, 573–593.

Marsh, H. (1992) "Extracurricular activities: beneficial extension of the traditional curriculum or subversion of academic goals?" *Journal of Educational Psychology 84*, 553–562.

Murray, J. (2005) "The Effects of Imprisonment on Families and Children of Prisoners." In A. Liebling and S. Maruna (eds) *The Effects of Imprisonment.* Cullompton: Willan.

Murray, J. (2007) "The cycle of punishment: social exclusion of prisoners and their children." *Criminology and Criminal Justice 7*, 55–81.

Murray, J. and Farrington, D.P. (2005) "Parental imprisonment: effects on boys' antisocial behaviour and delinquency through the life-course." *Journal of Child Psychology and Psychiatry 46*, 12, 1269–1278.

Murray, J. and Farrington, D.P. (2008) "Parental imprisonment: long-lasting effects on boys' internalizing problems through the life course." *Development and Psychopathology 20*, 273–290.

Murray, J., Farrington, D.P. and Sekol, I. (2012) "Children's Antisocial behavior, mental health, drug use, and educational performance after parental incarceration." *Psychological Bulletin 138*, 2, 175–210.

Nesmith, A. and Ruhland, E. (2008) "Children of incarcerated parents: challenges and resiliency, in their own words." *Children and Youth Services Review 30*, 1119–1130.

Parke, R.S. and Clarke-Stewart, K.A. (2003) "The Effects of Parental Incarceration on children: Perspectives, Promises and Policies." In J. Travis and M. Waul (eds) *Prisoners Once Removed.* Washington, DC: The Urban Institute Press.

Pew Charitable Trusts (2008) *1 in 100: Behind Bars in America 2008.* Washington, DC: Pew Charitable Trusts. Available at http://www.pewtrusts.org/our_work_report_detail.aspx?id=35900, accessed 5 October 2013.

Poehlmann, J., Park, J., Bouffiou, L., Abrahams, J., Shlafer, R. and Hahn, E. (2008) "Attachment representations in children raised by their grandparents." *Attachment and Human Development 10*, 165–188.

Richards, M., McWilliams, B., Allcock, L., Enterkin, J., Owens, P. and Woodrow, J. (1994) *The Family Ties of English Prisoners: The Results of the Cambridge Project on Imprisonment and Family Ties.* Cambridge: Centre for Family Research, University of Cambridge.

Tangney, J.P. and Dearing, R. (2002) *Shame and Guilt.* New York: Guilford.

Trice, A.D. and Brewster, J. (2004) "The effects of maternal incarceration on adolescent children." *Journal of Police and Criminal Psychology 19*, 27–35.

Walmsley, R. (2009) *World Prison Population List* (8th edition). London: International Centre for Prison Studies, King's College London.

Wildeman, C. (2009) "Paternal incarceration, the prison boom, and the concentration of disadvantage." *Demography 46*, 265–280.

CHAPTER 8

Families with a Substance-Abusing Child

Introduction

Alcohol and drug use among adolescents is a significant public health problem. Compared with adults, teens have higher rates of binge use and greater complications because of the developmental changes they are undergoing (Dennis 2002). Indeed, substance use/abuse among teens affects cognitive and emotional development, school performance and family relationships.

Research also suggests that young substance use onset is a risk factor for the development of a substance use disorder in adulthood. Ninety percent of adults diagnosed with substance abuse disorders reported that they started using before age 18; half of those reported beginning before age 15 (Dennis, 2002).

It is estimated that 11.9 percent of high school students meet the criteria for a substance use *disorder* (CASA 2009). Additional research showed 7 percent of 8th graders, 18 percent of 10th graders and 24 percent of 12th graders binge drank (defined as more than five drinks in a row) at least once during the two-week period prior to the survey. Males reported higher rates of daily drinking and binge drinking than females, and white students reported the highest levels of drinking. *Daily* marijuana use appears to be at the rate of 1 percent for 8th graders, 3.5 percent for 10th graders and 6.5 percent for 12th graders (Johnston *et al.* 2013).

There are many risk factors that contribute to substance abuse in adolescents, including:

- family history of substance use disorders
- antisocial behavior at a young age, especially aggression
- poor self-esteem
- school failure
- ADD and AD/HD
- learning disabilities

- peers who use drugs
- peer victimization or bullying
- alienation from peers or family
- depression and other mental health problems
- minority sexual identity
- a history of physical or sexual abuse (American Academy of Pediatrics 2001).

Of particular interest is the fact that in many families with a substance-abusing teen, there is also at least one parent who abuses substances (Alexander and Gwyther 1995). In addition, it is estimated that 60–80 percent of adolescents with substance-use disorders also have a co-occurring mental illness (Partnership for Drug Free America 2010).

Vulnerabilities

Drug/alcohol abuse plays a major role in teenage deaths, including homicide, suicide, traffic accidents and other injuries. Substance use among adolescents is also associated with poor school performance, problems with authority and high-risk behaviors such as unsafe sexual practices and driving while under the influence. Studies have shown that 15-year-olds who drink are also seven times more likely to have sexual intercourse than their nondrinking peers (American Academy of Pediatrics 2001).

Substance abuse among teens increases the risk for injuries, violence, sexually transmitted diseases and addiction (American Academy of Pediatrics 2001). It also can lead to delinquency, impulsivity, neurological impairment and developmental impairment (Alexander and Gwyther 1995; Center for Substance Abuse Treatment 1999).

Adolescents who abuse drugs/alcohol are more likely to interact primarily with peers who also abuse substances, so relationships and social skills may become dysfunctional. Impulsive and risk-taking behaviors are more pervasive in this population as well (Cuomo et al. 2008; Moeller and Dougherty 2002).

Families with troubled youth can often become hopeless and blaming in their perceptions of the problem (Coatsworth et al. 2001). Siblings may suffer. Indeed, parents may be reactive to the constant crises with the substance-abusing teen and ignore or minimize siblings' needs. Neglected siblings can then begin to misbehave themselves as a way to get attention.

Strengths

Often when families have a substance-abusing teen, there is access to many outside supports and resources through the school or community. These resources are not always available to other kinds of adolescent problems and can benefit both the teen and her/his family.

In addition, because adolescent substance abuse is a family crisis, families often pull together in order to address the problem. In many cases extended family members are also engaged, thereby increasing the family cohesion and support.

Empirical Support for Potential Treatment Approaches

More and more research supports family therapy as part of effective treatment for ameliorating adolescent drug use (Liddle and Dakof 1995). And, while 68 percent of teens with a substance use disorder also have a co-occurring disruptive behavior disorder, Bukstein (2000) emphasized that family therapy interventions are helpful for both disorders as they focus on environmental factors that support them.

Specific family therapy approaches, such as Brief Strategic Family Therapy and Multidimensional Family Therapy have shown great promise in reducing drug use and behavioral problems in adolescents and in improving family functioning (Hogue *et al.* 2004; Liddle *et al.* 2001; Szapocznik and Williams 2000). Both Brief Strategic Family Therapy and Multidimensional Family Therapy address:

- redirecting negative family communication patterns
- changing unhealthy family alliances
- developing conflict resolution skills
- developing effective behavior management
- teaching positive parenting.

Research also indicates that parental messages of disapproval of substance use is associated with lower rates of teen substance use (Brody *et al.* 1999). Indeed, parental silence can be perceived as passive support or as "not caring." When a parent openly discusses the risks of substance abuse it can reduce a teen's desire to experiment or ask their friends, who are often misinformed.

Resources

- Positive parenting tip sheet for teens from the Center for Disease Control (CDC): www.cdc.gov/ncbddd/childdevelopment/positiveparenting/pdfs/teen15-17.pdf

- Family check-up by the National Institute on Drug Abuse: www.drugabuse.gov/sites/default/files/files/Famliycheckupall.pdf

- Substance Abuse and Mental Health Services Administration (SAMHSA)'s drug use statistics by individual drugs: www.oas.samhsa.gov/drugs.cfm

- Above the Influence—a site for teens: www.abovetheinfluence.com

Counselor Cautions

Counselors need to be aware that adolescence is a period of multiple developmental changes. Not only do adolescents experience biological changes with hormonal systems, they also experience cognitive changes with a shift from concrete to abstract thinking. They are also moving from a family-based identity to a peer-based identity to an individually based identity. All of these development domains should be considered in treatment, along with gender and ethnicity issues.

Most adolescents will deny that drugs/alcohol are problematic and only enter treatment because they are forced to by parents. This often causes the need for multiple treatment episodes. It is important for counselors to work with the teens to find their own motivation to change and to develop strong therapeutic relationships with both the adolescent and her/his family.

When adolescents abuse substances, it is often the case that at least one parent also abuses substances (Alexander and Gwyther 1995). This dynamic of two or more substance abusers in the home means the family is vulnerable to experiencing additional physical and emotional problems. Counselors should be alert to parental substance abuse and be willing to address it if it arises.

Discussion Questions

- How has substance abuse affected your family?

- What things do you worry about regarding your substance-abusing adolescent?

- *<To parent(s) only>* Do you have a plan for what to do when your child comes home intoxicated?

- *<To substance-abusing adolescent only>* Do you feel comfortable calling your parent(s)/caregiver(s) if you are in a situation where you have been drinking or doing drugs and you need a ride home?

- *<To substance-abusing adolescent only>* Who do you feel comfortable calling if you are in a risky/dangerous situation?

- What things do you worry about regarding other family members?

- What two people have the most conflict in your family? What about the least conflict?

- What other treatment approaches are you using besides family therapy for your teen?

- On a scale of one to ten, with one being not at all and ten being a lot, how important do each of you think it is to change? And why not a *<insert a number lower than the number the family member has stated>*?

Ideas for Between-Session Homework

- Encourage the parent(s)/caregiver(s) to engage the adolescent's friends and to provide increased supervision.

- Encourage the family to do activities together—movie night, games night, meals together, visits to extended families, etc.

- Ask the family to research support groups in the area and to try one out.

- If appropriate, ask parents to research the use of "everyday" items that teens use in order to get high/drunk (i.e. drinking cough syrup, smoking duct tape, etc.).

- Ask family members to engage in individual nurturing self-care activities.

- Encourage the family to support the teen in the exploration of hobbies and interests.

- Assign one-on-one fun time between a parent/caregiver and siblings.

Therapeutic Activities

Activities included in this section are experiential opportunities to address typical but specific family issues related to adolescent substance abuse. Not all activities will apply to every family. Using their best clinical judgment, counselors should carefully select those activities that best address a specific teen's and family's problem(s).

HOW MUCH DO WE KNOW?

PARTICIPANTS
Parent/caregiver(s) and children (ages 11–18)

PURPOSE
To improve knowledge of substance abuse

MATERIALS

- Paper for scoring

- Pen or pencil

DESCRIPTION
Explain to the family that knowledge is power. Tell them that you will be reading random questions one by one about drugs and alcohol (see list of questions and answers below). If they think they know the answer to the question, they should quickly slap the table (ringers, whistles, etc. can also be used). The first person to slap the table gets an opportunity to answer the question. If s/he answers correctly s/he earns two points. If s/he answers incorrectly, s/he *loses* one point and the person who was second to slap the table gets an opportunity to answer the question. The family member with the most points wins.

Questions to be read:

1. What is a 12-step program?

   A support group that uses a set of 12 guiding principles that outline a plan for recovery from addiction.

2. What is the most commonly used drug by teens?

   Alcohol.

3. True or false? Teens who drink are more likely to be victims of violent crimes.

   True.

4. A teen is how many times more likely to develop alcohol *dependence* than someone who waits until adulthood to use alcohol?

   Four times.

5. Do more or fewer than 50 percent of teens say that alcohol is easy to get hold of?

   More (64 percent).

6. What kind of drug is alcohol?

   A depressant (meaning that it slows down functioning).

7. Approximately what percentage of physical injuries on college campuses are a result of alcohol?

   50 percent.

8. What are some of the physical symptoms of a hangover?

   Nausea, fatigue, upset stomach, headache, sore muscles, "cotton mouth."

9. What is alcohol tolerance?

   Needing increasing amounts of alcohol to feel the same effects.

10. Why do people drink?

    (Any of these responses is correct.) To unwind, to reward themselves, to fit in, to numb feelings, to feel less inhibited.

11. What has the greater effect on teens' choices to use alcohol: parent permissiveness or peer pressure?

    Parent permissiveness.

12. Do boys or girls become intoxicated faster?

    Girls.

13. What is binge drinking?

    The heavy consumption of alcohol over a short period of time. Four or more drinks in a row.

14. What are the signs of alcohol poisoning?

    (Any of these responses is correct.) Extreme confusion, inability to be awakened, vomiting, seizures, slow or irregular breathing, low body temperature, bluish or pale skin.

15. What should one do if s/he sees that someone has alcohol poisoning?

(Any and *all* of these responses are correct.) Call 911, turn the person on her/his side so s/he will not choke on vomit, stay with the person.

16. What's the difference between a social drinker (SD) and a problem drinker (PD)?

(Any of these responses is correct.) SD knows when to stop/PD drinks to get drunk; SD never drives while drinking/PD does; SD drinks slowly and with food/PD gulps drinks; SD maintains her/himself while drinking/PD may become loud, angry, violent or silent.

17. Are girls more likely to drink because of family problems or peer pressure?

Family problems.

18. What is the most widely illicit drug used in the United States?

Marijuana.

19. Name two street names for marijuana.

(Any of these responses is correct.) Pot, grass, weed, Mary Jane, reefer, skunk, dope, joint, boom, gangster, kif and ganja.

20. What is the name of the plant that marijuana comes from?

Cannabis.

21. Name one of the observable signs that someone is using marijuana.

(Any of these responses is correct.) Seems silly/giggly for no reason, has red/bloodshot eyes, seems dizzy and has trouble walking, has a hard time remembering things that just happened.

22. What is one immediate side effect of using marijuana?

(Any of these responses is correct.) Impaired short-term memory, perception, judgment and motor skills.

23. Name one street name for methamphetamines.

(Any of these responses is correct.) Speed, chalk, ice, crystal, crystal meth, jib, crank, croak, crypto, fire, glass, tweek, white cross.

24. What is one long-term effect of methamphetamine use?

(Any of these responses is correct.) Paranoia, hallucinations, repetitive behavior patterns, delusions of insects on the skin.

25. Name two observable features of a long-term user of methamphetamines.

(Any of these responses is correct.) Weight loss, strong body odor, shadows under the eyes, pale complexion, irritability, picking at skin, aggressive behavior, long periods of wakefulness.

26. Name one way that parents can prevent drug/alcohol abuse.

(Any of these responses is correct.) Good communication, being involved in teen's life, being a positive role model, having clear rules and enforcing them consistently, talking to teens about drugs.

DISCUSSION QUESTIONS

- How would you rate your family's knowledge of drugs and alcohol?

- What information surprised you?

- What information scared you?

- How did family members handle their frustrated feelings if they got a wrong answer?

- What do you think about the idea of playing games with your family?

ASSERTIVE COMMUNICATION

PARTICIPANTS

Parent/caregiver(s) and children (ages 8–18)

PURPOSE

To improve assertive communication and cooperation

MATERIALS

- Appendix E

- Scissors

DESCRIPTION

Prior to the family's arrival, make a photocopy of Appendix E, cut out the cards, mix them up and lay them face down on a table. Explain to the family that conflicts can be avoided when family members communicate *assertively* rather than passively or aggressively. Define passive, aggressive and assertive communication styles and *give examples*. Then divide the family into two teams, giving consideration to which family members should work together and which should not (i.e. avoid putting members on the same team where there is already an unhealthy alliance). Explain that the teams will take turns turning over the top card on the deck and deciding if the statement is passive, aggressive or assertive. Encourage consultation between team members before giving final responses. If correct, the team gets to keep the card. If incorrect, the team puts the card in a discarded pile. The team with the greatest number of cards at the end of the game wins.

DISCUSSION QUESTIONS

- How well did your team members work together?

- How did you handle frustrated feelings if your team got a wrong answer? Was there blaming and put-downs? Or was there consolation and support?

- Do members of your family tend to communicate in a passive, aggressive or assertive way?

- What do you think are the benefits of communicating in an assertive way?

- Were family members good sports when they lost the game? What would be an assertive way to express disappointment at not winning?

- What are some ways that your family could grow in its abilities to use assertive communication?

FAMILY IMPULSE CONTROL

PARTICIPANTS
Parent/caregiver(s) and children (ages 8–18)

PURPOSE
To increase impulse control and understanding of other family members

MATERIALS

- Appendix F
- Index cards
- Pens/pencils

DESCRIPTION
Prior to the family's arrival, cut out the cards from Appendix F and lay them face down on the table. When the family arrives, explain that impulse control is an important part of emotional intelligence and recovery from substance abuse. One way to practice impulse control is to stop and consider the consequences of a potential action. Hand each family member 10–18 blank index cards (depending on how long you want to play) and a pen or pencil. One at a time, ask a family member to draw a card and read it. S/he should then write down on an index card what s/he thinks might be one of the consequences if the stated impulse was acted upon. All the other family members should then write down on their cards what they think the *reader of the card* wrote. When all family members have finished writing, everyone shares their answers. If family members' answers match the answer of the *reader of the card* they get to keep their cards. If their answers do not match the *reader of the card,* they must discard their cards into a pile. The reader of the card gets to keep his/her card if anyone has matched her/his answer but must discard it if no one matches her/his answer. The person with the greatest number of cards at the end of the game wins.

DISCUSSION QUESTIONS

- How well did your family do *overall* in knowing what each other put down as consequences of impulsive behavior?

- How did it feel when family members guessed correctly what you wrote down?

- Did any of the situations on the cards seem like things that really happen in your family? Which ones?

- Why is impulse control an important skill to learn? How would it help your family?

- What are some things that you can do to improve your impulse control?

VALUES, VALUES, VALUES

PARTICIPANTS
Parent/caregiver(s) and children (ages 10–18)

PURPOSE
To increase motivation to change, identity and family differentiation

MATERIALS

- Values cards in Appendix G

- Scissors

- Pens/pencils

DESCRIPTION
Prior to the family's arrival, photocopy enough copies of the Values Cards from Appendix G so that each family member will have a complete set. Cut these out so that each family member will have 36 separate values cards. When the family arrives explain that values are those personal and moral principles that act as compasses in giving us direction. Then direct the family members to sort through their stack of Values Cards and pull out their own personal top five values (the things that are most important to them). Emphasize that individual values differ and there are no wrong answers. When everyone has selected their top five Values Cards, ask them to write on the backs of each:

1. One activity or behavior that they are engaged in that is consistent with or matches this value.

2. One activity or behavior that they are engaged in that is *not* consistent with this value.

For example, if one selects "beauty" as a value, it might be that s/he would state that s/he takes good care of her/his looks and clothing (matches) but doesn't clean her/his room regularly (*not* consistent). Then ask everyone to share their top five values and the activities/behaviors that are congruent and not congruent with those values.

DISCUSSION QUESTIONS

- Which values do you share with your other family members?

- Which single value seems to be valued by the greatest number of family members?

- Were you surprised at anyone's values?

- Where do you think your values come from? How did you adopt your values?

- Is it okay to have different values? How difficult is it to see where your family members differ?

- What did you learn about yourselves as you examined your activities/behaviors regarding your values? Were you inspired to change or do something differently?

SOLUTIONS WAR

PARTICIPANTS
Parent/caregiver(s) and children (ages 10–18)

PURPOSE
To decrease impulsivity and enhance problem-solving abilities

MATERIALS

- Deck of cards

DESCRIPTION
Explain to the family that impulsivity is doing the first thing that pops into your head without thinking about it. Explain that good problem-solving is the opposite of impulsivity because it requires generating multiple solutions to a situation/problem and evaluating each solution in order to find the best one. Explain that in this exercise the family will be playing the card game, War, but with a twist. Then shuffle the deck of cards and deal them so that each family member has the same number of cards. Family members should keep their cards in front of them, face down. Every family member then turns over her/his top card at the same time. The family member who has the lowest card must then describe a problem (this could be real or hypothetical; it could be about participation in family activities, failure to follow household rules, coping with stressful life events, etc.). The person with the highest card then must give three solutions to that problem. The problem-solver (or person with the highest card) then gets to take all the face-up cards and put them at the bottom of her/his face-down pile. In the event of a tie (two family members getting the same high card), they must place three cards face down in the middle of the table and then turn over a fourth card face up. The player with the higher of these cards becomes the player who gives solutions and takes the cards. Play as long as the family seems to be enjoying themselves or for a designated period of time (such as 20–30 minutes).

DISCUSSION QUESTIONS

- What do you do now when you have a conflict or problem?

- How difficult was it to come up with problems to solve?

- How difficult was it to come up with three solutions?

- Were there any solutions that you really liked?

- What solutions do you think will be the easiest for your family? Which will be the hardest? Why?

- Were there problems mentioned that you did not realize were problems?

- What do you think the benefits of this would be if you practiced it at school/ work? What about with your family?

UNDERNEATH ANGRY FEELINGS

PARTICIPANTS
Parent/caregiver(s) and children (ages 10–18)

PURPOSE
To increase self-awareness and decrease emotional reactivity

MATERIALS

- Paper

- Pens/pencils

DESCRIPTION
Explain to the family that anger is considered a secondary emotion— it follows a primary emotion. Understanding this and communicating the primary feeling rather than anger can produce better results in family conflicts. Ask each family member to put a vertical line down the middle of their paper. On the left side of the line direct them to write down five to ten incidents when they felt angry (i.e. "When my boss didn't give me the raise I deserved," or "When my sister went into my room without permission," etc.) Then, across from each situation on the right side of the page, direct them to write down the feeling word that describes what they felt a split second before the anger set in. If the family members have difficulty identifying appropriate feeling words, the counselor can write out some feelings words on a piece of paper for the family to refer to. Typical feelings that trigger anger include:

- embarrassed

- worried

- humiliated

- victimized

- left out

- cheated

- inadequate

- stupid

- nervous

- controlled

- put down

- confused

- helpless

- fearful

- sad

- surprised

- scared

- disappointed.

After everyone has completed their sheet, ask them to share what they have written.

DISCUSSION QUESTIONS

- Have angry feelings been a problem in your family? How?

- Were you surprised that other feelings trigger anger?

- What feeling seems to trigger anger the most in your family as a whole? What about as individuals?

- What can you do with this knowledge about anger?

- What would it be like if your family members talked about the feelings that trigger their anger rather than their angry feelings?

ROUND ROBIN "I" STATEMENTS

PARTICIPANTS
Parent/caregiver(s) and children (ages 8–18)

PURPOSE
To improve communication skills and personal responsibility

MATERIALS

- None

DESCRIPTION
Explain to the family that good communication means avoiding blaming, and expressing one's feelings calmly and directly—this can be done by making "I" statements. Explain that each person will turn to the person on her/his left and, using the template, "When

you _____ I feel _____ and I would like _____," will express a feeling to that particular family member. This can be a positive statement such as "When you help me with the dishes I feel supported and I would like for us to help each other more often" or it can be a more difficult statement such as "When you come in late after your curfew I feel terrified and I would like for you to be home on time." After the speaker has made her/his "I" statement, direct the listener to simply respond with "Thank you for sharing that." When everyone has both made and received an "I" statement, reverse the communication by having everyone use the template with the person on her/his *right*.

DISCUSSION QUESTIONS

- On a scale of one to ten (with one being very uncomfortable and ten being very comfortable) how comfortable were each of you *making* the "I" statements to family members?

- On a scale of one to ten (with one being very uncomfortable and ten being very comfortable) how comfortable were each of you *hearing* the "I" statements made towards you?

- What do you like or not like about communicating with "I" statements?

- Do you think making "I" statements would help lessen conflicts in your family?

SIZING UP SUPERVISION

PARTICIPANTS
Parent/caregiver(s) only

PURPOSE
To improve supervision and parental consistency

MATERIALS

- Paper
- Pen or pencil

DESCRIPTION
Explain to the family that supervision is an important part of parenting. While monitoring teens' behaviors and whereabouts is challenging, appropriate supervision helps parents stay involved and recognize problems. Using four pieces of paper, write each of the Four C's on separate sheets of paper: Clear Rules, Communication, Checking Up, and Compliments. Then brainstorm with the parent/caregiver(s) examples of how they can apply each one. Ask the the parent/caregiver(s) to write these ideas down on the appropriate pieces of paper. Here are some examples.

CLEAR RULES

- "No friends at the house without an adult at home."
- "Curfew is at _____ o'clock."

COMMUNICATION

- "I can talk to my child about the hazards of substance abuse."
- "I can call my child's friend's parents when s/he is making plans to go to their home."

CHECKING UP

- "I can call my child at various times of the day."
- "I can make sure that my child is where s/he says he is going to be."

COMPLIMENTS

- "I can thank my child for coming home on time."
- "I can tell my child s/he has done a good job with chores."

DISCUSSION QUESTIONS

- Which of the four C's do you think will be the easiest for you to implement? Which will be the most difficult?
- What are some ways that you can remain consistent with the ideas that you wrote down?
- What kinds of consequences do you use when rules are broken? Are these consequences age appropriate? Are they consistent?
- How can you stop yourself from arguing when implementing a consequence? How can you keep yourself calm?
- What are some ways that you can get to know your child's friends?
- How do you think that compliments and praise affect your child?

THE M&M GAME

PARTICIPANTS
Parent/caregiver(s) and children (ages 6–18)

PURPOSE
To improve communication and increase anger management

MATERIALS
Fun-size packs of M&Ms or a large bag of M&Ms

DESCRIPTION

Explain to the family that, while anger is simply an emotion, inappropriate behaviors that often accompany angry feelings can hurt family relationships. Learning to be the "boss" of angry feelings is always better than having angry feelings be the "boss" of us. Give each family member a fun-size pack of M&Ms or, 10–15 from a large bag, making sure that everyone has at least one of every color. Ask family members to sort their M&Ms by color. Using the guide below, ask family members to take turns sharing answers for each color M&M they have, trying not to repeat an answer that another family member has already given.

- For every *red* M&M that you have, name things that cause you to feel angry.

- For every *blue* M&M that you have, identify things that you can *do* to distract yourself from feeling angry.

- For every *green* M&M that you have, describe things that you can *tell yourself* in order to calm down.

- For every *orange* M&M that you have, describe times when you have successfully *controlled* your temper and *how you did it!*

- For every *brown* M&M that you have, describe *consequences* that you have experienced because of inappropriate displays of anger.

- For every *yellow* M&M that you have, tell a joke, riddle or funny story.

DISCUSSION QUESTIONS

- Which answers were hardest to think of? Which were the easiest?

- Were you surprised or interested by any of the answers that your family gave?

- Have you ever been afraid of anyone's anger? What happened?

- The word "anger" is one letter short of "danger." Do you agree?

- Why do we get angriest with the people that we love?

- What things did you learn from this activity?

- What things can you use when you are feeling angry next time?

Additional Activities That May be Helpful

- Sweet Sentiments in Chapter 3: Single-Parent Families with an Absent Parent (p.30)

- Communication Shutdown Matching Game in Chapter 4: Divorced/ Separated/Unmarried Families—Both parents available (p.40)

- Family Collage in Chapter 6: Families with Grandparents as Caregivers (p.79)

- The Feelings Game in Chapter 7: Families with an Incarcerated Loved One (p.91)

- A Bag of Coping in Chapter 10: Families with a Mentally Ill Parent (p.149)
- Thumb-ball Support in Chapter 12: Families in Grief (p.178)

References

Alexander, D.E. and Gwyther, R.E. (1995) "Alcoholism in adolescents and their families: family-focused assessment and management." *Pediatric Clinics of North America, 42*, 1, 217–234.

American Academy of Pediatrics (2001) "Alcohol use and abuse: a pediatric concern." *Pediatrics 108, 1,* 185–189.

Brody, G.H., Flor, D.L., Hollett-Wright, N., McCoy, J.K. and Donovan, J. (1999) "Parent-child relationships, child temperament profiles and children's alcohol use norms." *Journal of Studies on Alcohol 13,* 45–51.

Bukstein, O.G. (2000) "Disruptive behavior disorders and substance use disorders in adolescents." *Journal of Psychoactive Drugs 32,* 1, 67–79.

CASA (2009) *CASA Analysis of the National Household Survey on Drug Use and Health (NSDUH).* New York: CASA.

Center for Substance Abuse Treatment (1999) *Treatment of Adolescents With Substance Use Disorders. Treatment Improvement Protocol (TIP) Series 32. DHHS Publication No (SMA) 99-3283.* Rockville, MD: Substance Abuse and Mental Health Services Administration.

Coatsworth, J.D., Santisteban, D.A., McBride, C.K. and Szapocznik, J. (2001) "Brief Strategic Family Therapy versus community control: engagement, retention, and an exploration of the moderating role of adolescent symptom severity." *Family Process 40,* 3, 313–332.

Cuomo, C., Sarchiapone, M., Giannantonio, M.D., Mancini, M. and Roy, A. (2008) "Aggression, impulsivity, personality traits, and childhood trauma of prisoners with substance abuse and addiction." *American Journal of Drug and Alcohol Abuse 34,* 3, 339–345.

Dennis, M.L. (2002) *Treatment Research on Adolescents Drug and Alcohol Abuse: Despite Progress, Many Challenges Remain (Invited Commentary). Connection.* Washington, DC: Academy for Health Services Research and Health Policy.

Hogue, A., Liddle, H.A., Dauber, S. and Samuolis, J. (2004) "Linking session focus to treatment outcome in evidence-based treatments for adolescent substance abuse." *Psychotherapy: Theory, Research, Practice, Training 41,* 83–96.

Johnston, L.D., O'Malley, P.M., Bachman, J.G. and Schulenberg, J.E. (2013) *Monitoring the Future National Survey Results on Drug Use, 1975–2012. Volume I: Secondary School Students.* Ann Arbor: Institute for Social Research, The University of Michigan.

Liddle, H.A. and Dakof, G.A. (1995) "Efficacy of family therapy for drug abuse: promising but not definitive." *Journal of Marital and Family Therapy 21,* 4, 511–543.

Liddle, H.A., Dakof, G.A., Parker, K., Diamond, G.S., Barrett, K. and Tejeda, M. (2001) "Multidimensional family therapy for adolescent drug abuse: results of a randomized clinical trial." *American Journal of Drug and Alcohol Abuse 27,* 4, 651–688.

Moeller, F.G. and Dougherty, D.M. (2002) "Impulsivity and substance abuse: what is the connection?" *Addiction Disorder and Their Treatment 1,* 3–10.

Partnership for Drug Free America (2010) *Alcohol and Drug Problem Overview.* New York: Partnership for Drug Free America. Available at: www.drugfree.org/wp-content/uploads/2010/09/DrugAlcohol-Overview-PDF.pdf, accessed 5 October 2013.

Szapocznik, J. and Williams, R.A. (2000) "Brief strategic family therapy: twenty-five years of interplay among theory, research and practice in adolescent behavior problems and drug abuse." *Clinical Child and Family Psychology Review 3,* 2, 117–134.

CHAPTER 9

Families with Parent Substance Abuse

Introduction

In the United States from 2002–2007 approximately 7.3 million children under 18 years of age lived with a parent who was dependent on or abused alcohol. About 2.1 million children lived with a parent who was dependent on or abused illicit drugs (Substance Abuse and Mental Health Services Administration 2009). Although substance-abusing parents and their families are a diverse group, children in these families are at risk of a multitude of negative outcomes. There are several factors that influence the extent to which children of substance abusers are affected by their parents' substance abuse, including the:

- age of the child (i.e. when the parent became involved in substance abuse)
- type and severity of the substance abuse
- parent's ability to fulfill a healthy parenting role
- level of support from other adults
- child's temperament
- extent to which the family is socially isolated.

The parent's level of recovery and presence within the family system also influences how family treatment is utilized. The substance-abusing parent may or may not participate in family sessions. However, family members can gain a greater understanding of what they are experiencing and can increase their coping skills whether or not the substance-abusing parent's drug/alcohol problems are immediately resolved or whether or not s/he participates in family treatment.

A parent's individual recovery varies based on the type of drug used, the degree of substance abuse and the extent of the substance's short-term and long-term effects. Another complexity is the parent's engagement in treatment or stage of change. Prochaska, DiClemente and Norcross (1992) identified stages of change as:

- precontemplation—user not considering change
- contemplation—user ambivalent about change
- preparation—user has decided to change and begins planning for recovery
- action—user tries new behaviors but is not yet stable
- maintenance—user establishes new behaviors for the long term.

A major goal of family therapy is prevention, particularly in the multigenerational transmission of substance-abuse problems. Research shows that if one person in a family abuses alcohol or drugs, other family members have an increased risk of developing substance-abuse problems as well. In fact, the single most potent risk factor for a predisposition to substance use and psychological problems is a parent's substance-abusing behavior (Johnson and Leff 1999).

Potential Challenges/Vulnerabilities

Substance abusers' households are characterized by high conflict, negativism, poor communication patterns, fewer family activities and sometimes the abdication of parenting responsibilities (Chase, Deming and Wells 1998; Kumpfer and DeMarsh 1986; Sher *et al.* 1991; Stein, Riedel and Roteram-Borus 1999). For example, family finances may be limited due to spending on alcohol or drugs, family gatherings may be ruined because of drunken/high behaviors and supervision of children may be ignored/forgotten while intoxicated or under the influence. There is often impaired problem-solving on the part of the addict and resentment on the part of family members. Additional associated problems can also include job loss, incarceration, loss of child custody, domestic violence and physical health problems.

Other family problems can include parental inconsistency, unrealistic parental expectations and misdirected anger (Reilly 1992). Parenting requires complex decision-making and behaviors, often in emotionally charged situations. It is almost impossible for a parent who is under the influence to handle this kind of complexity with sensitivity to environmental cues, emotion regulation and good judgment.

Children of substance-abusing parents can feel guilty and responsible for their parent's substance-abuse problems. They may believe that they caused the addiction or that they can stop it in some way. Along with this, children can also become parentified. Parentification is a role reversal or blurred parent–child boundary where children take on inappropriate levels of instrumental or emotional responsibility in the family. The impact of parentification is its interference with a child's mastery of normal developmental tasks. Research shows that children of substance-abusing parents exhibit adjustment problems, depression, anxiety, low self-esteem and a tendency to develop substance-abuse problems themselves (Giglio and Kaufman 1990; Johnson and Leff 1999).

Strengths

When the substance-abuse problem is finally identified, families often pull together in order to address the issue. In some cases, extended family members are engaged, thereby increasing the family cohesion and support.

Although children with substance-abusing parents are at increased risk for negative consequences, positive outcomes have also been identified. Indeed, some children are quite resilient in the face of parent substance abuse (Hurcom et al. 2000). They develop personal strategies to handle stress and disruption, autonomy and abilities to tolerate ambiguity, and they use good judgment and take responsibility for their own actions (Wolin and Wolin 1993).

Empirical Support for Potential Treatment Approaches

It is well recognized that individual treatment of the substance-abusing parent alone is not enough. Family interventions are also needed, both for helping children cope with the behaviors of the substance-abusing parent and for helping parents better manage behaviorally disinhibited children (Fischer, Lyness and Engler 2010). Family treatment may also prevent substance abuse in other family members by correcting maladaptive family dynamics (Alexander, Robbins and Sexton 2000). Indeed, family functioning can subtly maintain an addiction or it can create an environment that supports recovery (Walitzer 1999).

Research indicates that children of alcoholics display better coping and psychological adjustment when there is greater parent support and consistent discipline (Smith et al. 2006). Two programs—Families Facing the Future and Family Behavior Therapy for Adults—show evidence for reduced parent use of illegal drugs and decreased family dysfunction. While there is some variation in these programs, both include components of family goal setting, relapse prevention, communication skills and child management skills (Donohue and Azrin 2011; Haggerty et al. 2008). Research has also shown that children who have social competence and self-regulation skills are better able to make positive adjustments (Eisenberg et al. 2005; Spinrad et al. 2007).

Behavioral couples therapy is also an intervention that has shown positive outcomes. O'Farrell and Fals-Stewart (2000) found that behavioral couples therapy led to more drug/alcohol abstinence, decreased separation and divorce, and reduced domestic violence. Techniques in this manualized treatment are behavioral assignments designed to increase positive feelings, shared activities and constructive communication.

Resources

- *Children of Alcoholics* factsheet (published by American Academy of Child and Adolescent Psychiatry): www.aacap.org/App_Themes/AACAP/docs/facts_for_families/17_children_of_alcoholics.pdf

- *Children of Addicted Parents: Important Facts* (published by National Association for Children of Alcoholics): www.nacoa.net/pdfs/addicted.pdf

- Al-Anon and Alateen: www.al-anon.alateen.org

Counselor Cautions

Counselors can experience negative countertransference with parents in substance-abusing relationships. While this is not unusual, it does interfere with effective treatment. Counselors should examine their own attitudes, experiences and biases related to alcohol and/or drug abuse in order to maintain objectivity. Self-reflection and a basic understanding of addiction and its impact on individuals and families can help.

Substance abusers often have "denial" or "resistance" in the early stages of change. Counselors should see this as a normal response to feeling pressured to give up drugs and/or alcohol when the client is not ready to change. According to Kennedy and Charles (1990) reluctant clients often use defensive measures to avoid the painful work of change. These defensive behaviors often include silence combined with hostile body language and constantly questioning the competence of the therapist. Again, it is important for counselors to avoid personalizing these behaviors and to maintain an objective, therapeutic stance. The counselor can reduce resistance by avoiding strong confrontive statements such as "So you're refusing to _____," and should consider statements like, "Let's examine the pros and cons of _____."

If a child or family member is venting about their substance-abusing loved one, counselors should remember simply to listen and not join in. It may be tempting as part of rapport building to speak negatively about an absent or abusive parent, but there is still loyalty among family members. It may be tolerable for *them* to speak negatively about their loved one but not for *you!*

Discussion Questions

- How has substance abuse affected your family?

- What do you worry about regarding your substance-abusing parent/partner?

- What do you worry about regarding other family members?

- Are there things that you do in the family or roles that you have taken on that feel overwhelming? Who do you wish would help you?

- What are the best and worst times of day for your family? Why do you think this is true?

- What two people have the most conflict in your family? What about the least conflict?

- Do people have to agree on something in order to get along? What does it mean to agree to disagree?

- Who are the people outside of your family who you can call when you need support?

Ideas for Between-Session Homework

- Families with a substance-abusing parent often have multiple problems (i.e. incarceration, joblessness, domestic violence, etc.). Referrals for health care, job training, anger management, etc. are often needed and can be assigned as homework.

- Spirituality is often an important aspect of recovery from substance abuse. Families need to be encouraged and supported in their efforts to find a comfortable spiritual home.

- Families can be assigned the creation of a Calm Carrier. Using any kind of a bag or small suitcase, family members should be directed to fill it with self-care items such as stress balls, cartoons, bubbles, small stuffed animals, affirmations written on cards, etc. This can be brought to sessions or simply used at home as needed.

- If working with couples, ask each partner to "Catch Your Partner Doing Something Nice" daily. This means that couples acknowledge verbally to each other something that the other one did that was pleasing—every day for a week.

- Many substance-abusing families have stopped doing fun things together. Ask the family to plan and engage in a rewarding activity.

- Have the family create a safety plan for times when family members are frightened. This should include a safe place in the home, a list of telephone numbers, a safe place to go if necessary, what to do in various kinds of emergencies, etc.

Therapeutic Activities

Activities included in this section are experiential opportunities to address typical but specific family issues related to parent substance abuse. Not all activities will apply to every family. Using their best clinical judgment, counselors should carefully select those activities that best address a specific family's problem(s).

GENOGRAM

PARTICIPANTS
Parent/caregiver(s) and children (ages 6–18)

PURPOSE

To assist families in seeing addiction in a less blaming and shameful way

MATERIALS

- Paper
- Pencil

DESCRIPTION

Using the basic symbols of a genogram (see Chapter 2)—i.e. squares for males, circles for women, single horizontal lines for marriage etc—ask the family to give you information about extended family members so that you can create a genogram. Ask about any problems that may be multi-generational. Other information that can be recorded includes family alliances, family conflicts, emotional cut-offs, etc.

DISCUSSION QUESTIONS

- As you look at this genogram, what strikes you first?
- Do you see any patterns (i.e. illness, names, violence, alcohol, drugs)? What do you think this means?
- What new information did you learn about your family? Was anything surprising?
- What do you see as your family's strengths? What do you see as your family's weaknesses?
- Which things have been passed down to each of you?
- Which relationships are strong? Which relationships are weak?
- How do members of this family support each other?

FAMILY CHANGES

PARTICIPANTS

Parent/caregiver(s) and children (ages 6–18)

PURPOSE

To identify family goals for change

MATERIALS

- Paper
- Crayons or markers

DESCRIPTION

Explain to the family that in order for things to change, it is important to have goals—or a sense of direction. Hand each family member two sheets of paper. Ask them to use one sheet to draw a picture showing the family as they currently see it and the other sheet to draw a picture of how they would *like* the family to be. Ask family members to share their drawings.

DISCUSSION QUESTIONS

- How did you feel drawing the first picture of how your family is now?
- How did you feel drawing the second picture of how you would like your family to be?
- How were your pictures similar to each other's? How were they different?
- Is it okay for family members to have different opinions?
- As you turn your paper over from how your family is now to how you want it to be, what behavior changes do each of you need to make to "turn over a new leaf" in your family?
- Who do you think will be the first one to make these changes?
- How can counseling help your family make these changes?

A STRAND OF ANGELS

PARTICIPANTS
Parent/caregiver(s) and children (ages 6–18)

PURPOSE
To recognize support persons and to create a reference of safe people to reach out to

MATERIALS

- Paper
- Scissors
- Pens/pencils
- Glue stick

DESCRIPTION
Prior to the session, cut out several angel shapes from blank pieces of paper. Then, during the session, explain to the family that human "angels" are real people who come into our lives to help us. Their words or actions comfort us, remind us to do our best, help us cope or see us through difficult situations. Ask family members to write down the names of people in their lives (one name per angel) who have influenced them in a positive way or been an "angel." Glue the angels together so that they make a strand of angels and then naming each one, ask family members to state why each one was listed. Afterwards, direct the family to take the strand of angels home and to hang it in a central location. Optional: add phone numbers under each name.

DISCUSSION QUESTIONS

- What strikes you about your strand of "angels" as you look at it?

- Were there any disagreements among you about who to include and who not to include as an angel?

- Who in the family could easily think of names of "angels?" Who had a harder time thinking of "angels?"

- Do you know how to get in touch with one of your "angels" if you need to?

- Do you have a favorite "angel"?

- Have you ever been an "angel" for someone else?

DIFFICULT FEELINGS

PARTICIPANTS
Parent/caregiver(s) and children (ages 6–18)

PURPOSE
To identify difficult feelings and create dialogue about feelings and substance abuse

MATERIALS

- Paper
- Pens/pencils
- Crayons/markers

DESCRIPTION
Explain to the family that difficult feelings are those feelings that we often avoid because they can be painful, frightening or overwhelming. If needed, provide a general list of feelings words and point out a few feelings that others have found difficult to talk about (i.e. shamed, frightened, etc.) Then hand each family member two sheets of paper. Ask them to make a brief list of *their* difficult feelings on one sheet. Then ask them to select one of those feelings and, on the second sheet of paper, draw one of the feelings on their list that they felt during a situation when their loved one was abusing drugs/alcohol. Ask the family members to share the pictures with each other.

DISCUSSION QUESTIONS

- How easy or hard was it for you to share your picture and talk about your uncomfortable feeling?

- What makes some feelings harder to talk about than others?

- How does your family handle it when members try to talk about feelings in general?

- Were you surprised by other family members' feelings or pictures?

- Since we did this exercise, do you think it will be easier to talk about your uncomfortable feeling the next time you experience it?

- Besides talking, what else can you do to make yourself feel better when you have uncomfortable feelings?

BOARD GAME FOR SUBSTANCE ABUSE

PARTICIPANTS
Parent/caregiver and children (ages 6 and up)

PURPOSE
To improve communication, frustration tolerance and cohesion

MATERIALS

- Snakes and Ladders board game

- Appendix A cards (feelings, interactions and discussions)

- Appendix H cards (substance abuse)

DESCRIPTION
Make photocopies of the four sets of game cards (Appendices A and H) using four different colors of copy paper (or simply write "Substance Abuse," "Discussion," "Interactions" and "Feelings" on the backs of the appropriate cards). Then play Snakes and Ladders (moving up or down the board if you land on a ladder or a snake) with a difference—when players land on a numbered space they must answer a question from one of the four sets of cards. If they land on numbers 1–25 they should answer a "Substance Abuse" card; if they land on numbers 26–50 they should answer a "Discussion" card; if they land on numbers 51–75 they should answer a "Interactions" card; if they land on numbers 76–100 they should answer a "Feelings" card. The first player to reach the top wins.

DISCUSSION QUESTIONS

- Were the questions on any one set of cards harder or easier to answer? Why?

- How do you feel now that the game is over and you have answered all these questions? How do you feel about yourself? How do you feel about your family members?

- What was the experience of simply playing a game together like?

- What questions would you like to add to the game?

- What did you learn about yourself? What did you learn about your family members?

- Did anything in the game inspire you to want to change something in yourself or in your family?

MAKING "I" STATEMENTS

PARTICIPANTS
Parent/caregiver(s) and children (ages 6–18)

PURPOSE
To practice effective communication patterns and assertiveness

MATERIALS
- Paper
- Pens/pencils
- Crayons/markers

DESCRIPTION
Explain to the family that "You" statements are blaming and that "I" statements take responsibility for one's own feelings. Then direct family members to pair up and ask each person to make these four "I" statement to their partners.

1. "I felt happy when you _____."
2. "I felt sad when you _____."
3. "I felt angry when you _____."
4. "I felt scared when you _____."

Get the family members to form new pairs and repeat the activity.

DISCUSSION QUESTIONS
- How did you feel making "I" statements?
- Which of the four feelings was most difficult for you to express?
- How did you feel hearing your partners' "I" statements to you?
- How would things be different in your family if family members communicated using more "I" statements?
- Why do you think it's important to use "I" statements?

PARENTING CONSISTENCY

PARTICIPANTS
Parent/caregiver(s)

PURPOSE
To increase parent consistency and boundary setting

MATERIALS

- Paper
- Pen or pencil

DESCRIPTION
Explain to the caregiver(s) that because of addiction, family life often becomes chaotic, inconsistent and unpredictable. Rules and roles are unclear because they are forever changing based on the addict's state of intoxication and other family members' reactivity. Explain that consistency in parenting is one of the most important aspects in producing children who are emotionally stable. Clarify that rules and consequences need to remain consistent, no matter what the circumstances are. Then ask the caregiver(s) to describe five child behaviors that are unacceptable to her/him. From these behaviors, assist the caregiver(s) in creating five rules and write these on the left side of a piece of paper. Then brainstorm logical and developmentally appropriate consequences for each infraction of a rule and write these on the right side of the page across from the rule.

DISCUSSION QUESTIONS

- How do you feel about the work that you just did?

- What might be some of the obstacles to sticking with this plan? How can you manage those obstacles in order to increase success?

- Which of these rules and consequences will be the easiest to implement? Which will be the most difficult?

- Describe a time when you were consistent with a rule and its consequence. How were you able to do it?

- Who do you know who is a consistent parent? How do you think s/he does it? Is this someone you can talk to and get support from?

- How will you present this to the children? Would you like to do this in or out of our sessions?

WHAT MIGHT HAPPEN

PARTICIPANTS

Parent/caregiver(s) and children (ages 6–18)

PURPOSE

To increase impulse control and acknowledge boundaries

MATERIALS

- Jenga game

DESCRIPTION

Prior to the family's arrival, write down the following phrases on Jenga blocks—one phrase per block. Add any others that you think might be relevant for the family.

1. Talk back to my teacher/boss.

2. Eat a piece of pie saved for someone else.

3. Borrow someone else's game without asking permission.

4. Make a mean face when I'm angry.

5. Break something when I'm angry.

6. Interrupt someone while s/he is talking.

7. Blurt out an answer before the question is finished.

8. Jump into an activity with others without being invited.

9. Look inside someone else's purse.

10. Steal sweets from a shop.

11. Yell at someone when I'm angry.

12. Pick a flower out of a neighbor's yard without permission.

13. Cheat on a test.

14. Keep an unhealthy secret.

15. Laugh at someone who fell over.

16. Try to pet a strange dog.

17. Laugh at someone who just got in trouble.

18. Climb on the roof to get a kite that is stuck.

19. Call someone a bad name because they gave me a mean look.

20. Stay up late watching TV on a school/work night.

21. Skip a chore.

22. Sneak a peak at a wrapped gift that is for me.

23. Whine and complain when I'm bored.

24. Change the TV channel while someone is watching a show.

25. Spit out some food that tastes bad at a friend's house.

26. Tear up a project because I'm frustrated with it.

27. Brag about being allowed to do something.

28. Jump out of a tree.

29. Insist on going first in a game.

30. Throw the game board when I lose.

31. Hug someone I just met.

32. Grab the first piece of pizza when it is delivered.

33. Not wash my face.

34. Push someone who is in my way.

35. Say "That's stupid" to someone's idea.

36. Pinch someone and pretend someone else did it.

37. Cut in line.

38. Lie about something I did wrong.

39. Kick the dog because he's in my way.

40. Run through the house.

41. Eat a whole bag of sweets.

42. Spit at someone.

43. Run into the street.

44. Walk away from a drink I spilled.

45. Make a rude gesture at a driver that cut us off in traffic.

46. Make fun of my friend's new outfit.

47. Make fun of a family member's new haircut.

48. Burp loudly at the dinner table.

Explain to the family that using impulse control (the ability to stop and think) can help everyone better handle their feelings and get along better. One of the ways to improve impulse control is to think about the consequences of an impulse, which is what they will be doing in this game. Then stack the Jenga blocks into a tower according to the directions inside the game. Instruct the family to one at a time (with the youngest family member going first) use one hand and pull out a single block from the tower. They should then read the impulse on the block and describe the consequence(s) if s/he followed the impulse and what a better choice might be. Then the family member should restack the block at the top of the tower perpendicular to the layer of blocks beneath it. Continue until the tower falls.

Variation: You can simply write numbers 1–48 on Jenga blocks and have a sheet of paper with the numbered impulses. When the family member calls out the number on the block that s/he has selected, the counselor can read the same numbered impulse.

DISCUSSION QUESTIONS

- Everyone has impulses—do you think that you are the boss of your impulses or are your impulses the boss of you?

- The secret to impulse control is to stop and think before acting—what are some ways you can get yourself to *stop* before you decide what to do in a situation?

- How do you think improving impulse control will help your family?

- Can you name some times when you had the impulse to do something but you stopped yourself? How did you do it?

- Lots of people are impulsive when they're emotional. What kinds of things can you do to calm yourself when you're upset?

WALKING FOR SOLUTIONS

PARTICIPANTS
Parent/caregiver(s) and children (ages 6–18)

PURPOSE
To increase cooperation, impulse control and problem-solving skills

MATERIALS

- Index cards
- Pens/pencils
- Music

DESCRIPTION
Explain to the family that conflicts are often better resolved if several solutions are generated and considered before acting on one. Hand each family member three index cards and a pen or pencil. Ask them to write down one problem on each card so that each family member has identified three problems in total. These can be personal problems or family problems (i.e. "I'm having trouble in maths" or "We all seem to argue at the dinner table."). After everyone has written down their problems, collect them and mix them up. Then place the index cards face down on the floor in a large circle in the center of the room, leaving plenty of space between each card. Have family members stand on one of the cards in the circle and explain to them that you will be playing music for a few seconds/minutes as they walk around the circle using the

index cards as "stepping stones." When the music stops, everyone should stop. The person standing closest to the door should pick up the card that s/he is standing on, read the problem, give one solution for it and then call on two other family members to add additional solutions (so that there are three solutions in total). That problem card is then removed and the music starts again. The process is repeated until all of the problems on the index cards have been addressed. (As fewer and fewer cards are left on the floor, instruct the family that it is not necessary to jump from card to card but simply to walk in a circle even if they are not stepping on a card.)

DISCUSSION QUESTIONS

- How well did you cooperate when you were walking on the cards in a circle?
- Why is coming up with several solutions to a problem a good idea?
- How easy or difficult was it for you to come up with solutions?
- Do you think you'll use any of the solutions that you came up with today?
- What was it like to ask other family members to help with solutions?
- When do you think you could use this skill in the future?

COUPLE'S COMMUNICATION POKER

PARTICIPANTS
Adult couple

PURPOSE
To increase communication, playfulness and positive behaviors

MATERIALS

- 20 strips of paper
- Pens/pencils
- Deck of cards

DESCRIPTION
Hand each partner ten strips of paper and a pen or pencil. Ask them to write down ten specific, concrete and *doable* things that they would like from their partner (for example, cuddle time, fold the laundry, dinner alone without the kids, flowers, wash the car etc.). Then have them fold these strips two or three times so that they are square and the writing cannot be seen. These will serve as poker chips. Before each hand of poker, each partner antes or puts in one of the papers. The winner of the hand collects both papers. Allow play to continue for 15 minutes and then ask the partner with the *fewest* papers to read the papers that s/he possesses, beginning with the ones that s/he wrote. Have the couple discuss these for a few minutes. Then ask her/him to read

the ones that her/his partner wrote. Discuss again. Then have the partner with the *most* papers do the same. Then have each partner ask the other, "Of the papers that I have of yours, which one would you like me to do this week?" Encourage the couple to follow through with these behaviors as homework.

DISCUSSION QUESTIONS

- Was it difficult coming up with ten wishes? Why or why not?

- Were you surprised by any of your partner's wishes?

- What did you learn about yourself in this exercise?

- What did you learn about your partner in this exercise?

- What was it like to play together—even for just 15 minutes?

- How likely are you to follow through with your homework from this activity?

Additional Activities That May be Helpful

- Sweet Sentiments in Chapter 3: Single-Parent Families with an Absent Parent (p.30)

- Communication Shutdown Matching Game in Chapter 4: Divorced/ Separated/Unmarried Families (p.40)

- My Superhero Cape in Chapter 4: Divorced/Separated/Unmarried Families—Both parents available (p.45)

- It's Not My Fault in Chapter 4: Divorced/Separated/Unmarried Families— Both parents available (p.46)

- The Feelings Game in Chapter 7: Families with an Incarcerated Loved One (p.91)

- A Bag of Coping in Chapter 10: Families with a Mentally Ill Parent (p.148)

- Thumb-ball Support in Chapter 12: Families in Grief (p.178)

References

Alexander, J.F., Robbins, M.S. and Sexton, T.L. (2000) "Family-based interventions with older, at risk youth: from promise to proof to practice." *The Journal of Primary Prevention 21*, 2, 185–205.

Chase, N.D., Deming, M.P. and Wells, M.C. (1998) "Parentification, parental alcoholism, and academic status among young adults." *American Journal of Family Therapy 26*, 2, 105–114.

Donohue, B. and Azrin, N.H. (2011) *Family Behavior Therapy: A Step-by-step Approach to Adult Substance Abuse*. Hoboken, NJ: John Wiley and Sons.

Eisenberg, N., Zhou, Q., Spinrad, T.L., Valiente, C., Fabes, R.A. and Liew, J. (2005) "Relations among positive parenting, children's effortful control and externalizing problems: a three-wave longitudinal study." *Child Development 76*, 1055–1071.

Fischer, J., Lyness, K.P. and Engler, R. (2010) "Families Coping with Alcohol and Substance Abuse." In S.J. Price, C.A. Price and P.C. McKenry (eds) *Families and Change: Coping with Stressful Events and Transitions*. Thousand Oaks, CA: Sage Publications.

Giglio, J.J. and Kaufman, E. (1990) "The relationship between child and adult psychopathology in children of alcoholics." *International Journal of the Addictions 25*, 3, 263–290.

Haggerty, K.P., Skinner, M.L., Fleming, C.B., Gainey, R.R. and Catalano, R.F. (2008) "Long-term effects of the Focus on Families project on substance use disorders among children of parents in methadone treatment." *Addiction 103*, 2008–2016.

Hurcom, C., Copello, A. and Orford, J. (2000) "The family and alcohol: effects of excessive drinking and conceptualizations of spouses over recent decades." *Substance Use and Misuse 35*, 473–502.

Johnson, J.L. and Leff, M. (1999) "Children of substance abusers: overview of research findings." *Pediatrics 103*, 5,1085–1099.

Kennedy, E. and Charles, S.C. (1990) *On Becoming a Counselor: A Basic Guide for Non-professional Counselors*. New York: Continuum.

Kumpfer, K.L. and DeMarsh, J. (1986) "Family Environmental and Genetic Influences on Children's Future Chemical Dependency." In S. Griswold-Ezekoye, K.L. Kumpfer and W.J. Bukoski (eds) *Childhood and Chemical Abuse: Prevention and Intervention*. New York: Haworth Press.

O'Farrell, T.J. and Fals-Stewart, W. (2000) "Behavioral couples therapy for alcoholism and drug abuse." *Journal of Substance Abuse Treatment 18*, 1, 51–54.

Prochaska, J.O., DiClemente, C.C. and Norcross, J.C. (1992) "In search of how people change: applications to addictive behaviors." *American Psychologist 47*, 9,1102–1114.

Reilly, D.M. (1992) "Drug-Abusing Families: Intrafamilial Dynamics and Brief Triphasic Treatment." In E. Kaufman and P. Kaufmann (eds) *Family Therapy of Drug and Alcohol Abuse* (2nd edition). Boston: Allyn and Bacon.

Sher, K.J., Walitzer, K.S., Wood, P.K. and Brent, E.E. (1991) "Characteristics of children of alcoholics: putative risk factors, substance use and abuse, and psychopathology." *Journal of Abnormal Psychology 100*, 4, 427–448.

Smith, C.L., Eisenberg, N., Spinrad, T.L., Chassin, L., Sheffield-Morris, A., Kupfer, A., Liew, J., Cumberland, A., Valiente, C. and Kwok, O. (2006) "Children's coping strategies and coping efficacy: relations to parent socialization, child adjustment, and familial alcoholism." *Development and Psychopathology 18*, 445–469.

Spinrad, T.L., Eisenberg, N., Gaertner, B., Popp, T., Smith, C.L., Kupfer, A., Greving, K., Liew, J. and Hofer, C. (2007) "Relations of maternal socialization and toddlers' effortful control to children's adjustment and social competence." *Developmental Psychology 43*, 1170–1186.

Substance Abuse and Mental Health Services Administration (SAMHSA) (2009) *Children, Parents and Substance Abuse*. Rockville, MD: SAMHSA. Available at www.samhsa.gov/samhsanewsletter/Volume_17_Number_3/ParentsDrugs.aspx, accessed 6 October 2013.

Stein, J.A., Riedel, M. and Roteram-Borus, M.J. (1999) "Parentification and its impact on adolescent children of parents with AIDS." *Family Process 38*, 2, 193–208.

Walitzer, K.S. (1999) "Family Therapy." In P.J. Ott, R.E. Tarter and R.T. Ammerman (eds) *Sourcebook on Substance Abuse: Etiology, Epidemiology, Assessment, and Treatment*. Needham Heights, MA: Allyn and Bacon.

Wolin, S. J. and Wolin, S. (1993) *Bound and Determined: Growing Up Resilient in a Troubled Family*. New York: Vilfard Press.

CHAPTER 10

Families with a Mentally Ill Parent

Introduction

The National Alliance on Mental Health (2013a) defines a mental illness as:

> a medical condition that disrupts a person's thinking, feeling, mood, ability to relate to others and daily functioning. Just as diabetes is a disorder of the pancreas, mental illnesses are medical conditions that often result in a diminished capacity for coping with the ordinary demands of life.

Approximately 61.5 million Americans—the equivalent of one in four adult—experience mental illness in a given year (National Alliance on Mental Health 2013b).

The severity of clients' symptoms, as well as their ability to cope with a disorder, are influenced by social, psychological and biological factors (Schock-Giordano and Gavazzi 2005). Research suggests that a key feature for mentally ill persons' successful adjustment to the community is family support (Cherromas, Clarke and Marchinko 2008). However, many families report feeling discouraged and fatigued with their caregiving roles. Client behavior problems disrupt family structure and functioning, often leading to the emotional isolation of families (Cavaiola 2000).

Of those with a mental disorder, 51 percent reported at least one addictive disorder as well (Kessler *et al.* 1994). Co-occurring mental illness and substance abuse are associated with more negative outcomes than mental illness only (i.e. relapse, incarceration, homelessness, etc.) (Caton *et al.* 1994; De Leon, Sacks and Wexler 2002; Swofford *et al.* 1996).

Gender differences are associated with vulnerability to certain mental health disorders. Women have higher rates of affective and anxiety disorders, whereas men have higher rates of substance abuse, impulse control and antisocial personality disorders (Schock-Giordano and Gavazzi 2005; Kessler *et al.* 2005; Regier *et al.* 1988). Only half of all Americans who suffer from a serious mental illness seek treatment, although women are more likely to seek treatment than men (Kessler *et al.* 2001).

Potential Challenges/Vulnerabilities

Coping with a family member's mental illness frequently results in adverse effects for family members' physical and psychological health (Heru 2000; Fadden, Bebbington and Kuipers 1987). Children who have a parent with a major mental illness are at risk for emotional, behavioral and intellectual difficulties, developmental delays, school achievement problems, deficits in social functioning and drug and alcohol abuse later in life (Clarke and Annunziata 2006) and are at a higher risk for developing mental illness than other children (American Academy of Children and Adolescent Psychiatry 2008).

Mentally ill individuals experience stigma where shame outweighs even their most extreme psychiatric symptoms (Byrne 2000). Stigma-by-association or courtesy stigma has also been found to adversely affect family members' ability to cope effectively and is associated with psychologically distancing from the stigmatized relative (Bos *et al.* 2013).

Individuals living with serious mental illness face an increased risk for chronic medical conditions (National Alliance on Mental Health 2013b). Some of these conditions result from the mental illness itself, some as a consequence of treatment and some from unhealthy lifestyles (i.e. poor eating and sleeping habits, poor nutrition, etc.).

If a mentally ill person has children, the mental illness can make it difficult to parent and provide children with a stable and safe environment. It may be difficult to set limits and boundaries for them because of the parent's own confusion. S/he may also be less emotionally available for their child (Clarke and Annunziata 2006).

Strengths

Families with a mentally ill parent can be extremely resourceful. Children in these families may have advanced daily living skills, as they have been required to learn these skills at an early age. If the parent is involved in treatment, this is likely to open up other avenues of resources for the family.

Parents that have learned to successfully advocate for themselves can utilize these skills in other facets of family life—for example, advocating for their child who suffers from symptoms of ADHD. Their experience with mental illness may also allow them the knowledge base in order to teach their children appropriate coping skills, reactions to bullying and how to ask for help.

Empirical Support for Treatment

Systems theory posits that the mentally ill family member both affects the family and is affected by the family (Heru 2000). Indeed, research shows that patients with mental illness fare better when there is family intervention—patients with schizophrenia and bipolar disorder had lower relapse/rehospitalization rates and improved medication adherence with programs that included family therapy and family psychoeducation (Miklowitz *et al.* 2007; Pfammatter, Junghan and Brenner

2006; Rea *et al.* 2003). Miller *et al.* (2005) found that family therapy combined with antidepressant medication showed a more rapid recovery in patients with major depression than antidepressants combined with cognitive therapy.

New research on expressed emotion (EE) has found that mentally ill individuals who live with high EE (over-involved, critical or hostile) family members are more likely to relapse than persons with the same illness with low EE families (e.g. Miklowitz 2007). Barrowclough and Hooley (2003) suggest that this may be due to the fact that high EE families tend to blame the mentally ill individual for their abnormal behaviors, whereas low EE families seem to understand that the loved one's behavior is out of their control and simply a part of the mental illness.

Risk factors for children of mentally ill parents, including emotional, behavioral and intellectual difficulties, are reduced when they learn the facts about mental illness and receive emotional support and understanding from a mental health professional (Clarke and Annunziata 2006). Information for children should be presented clearly and directly, and in a way that is appropriate for the child's maturity level and age.

Research has shown that therapeutic intervention, including individual, group or family therapy, support groups or bibliotherapy help children tremendously (Clarke and Annunziata 2006). Therapy allows children to express their thoughts and feelings and to realize that they are not alone in their experience. Protective factors for children of mentally ill parents include:

- knowledge that their parent(s) is ill and that they are not to blame

- help and support from family members

- a stable home environment

- a sense of being loved by the ill parent

- inner strength and good coping skills in the child

- a strong relationship with a healthy adult

- friendships and positive peer relationships (American Academy of Children and Adolescent Psychiatry 2008).

Resources

- National Alliance on Mental Illness: www.nami.org

- *Facts for Families: Children of Parents with Mental Illness*: www.aacap.org/App_Themes/AACAP/docs/facts_for_families/39_children_of_parents_with_mental_illness.pdf

- American Psychological Association: www.apa.org

- National Institute of Mental Health: www.nimh.nih.gov

Counselor Cautions

When utilizing psychoeducation, it is important to make sure that you are utilizing age-appropriate material and language in order to avoid confusing child/ren and intensifying their stress. If there is a spouse involved in treatment, do not assume that s/he already knows everything about their significant other's mental illness. Be prepared to provide psychoeducation for her/him as well.

Working with a parent suffering from a mental illness can be difficult. Depending on her/his symptom severity, counselors must recognize that follow-through may not be possible for the mentally ill family member. This must be considered when developing strategies to accomplish treatment goals. In some cases it may be necessary to complete activities during sessions rather than assigning them for homework.

When working with these families, it is important to inquire about the child/ren's emotional development and mental health. Because children of a mentally ill parent have a higher risk for developing mental illnesses themselves, it is important to address any concerns that you may observe and discuss the possibility of having the child evaluated for treatment as well.

Discussion Questions

- What are your family's strengths?

- What do you know about your loved one's mental illness?

- Do you have any questions about your loved one's mental illness?

- What are the resources that you rely on? Are there others that you need?

- Who are your supports? Is there someone that you can call in the middle of the night if you need to?

- Are you ever nervous about talking about your mentally ill loved one to others?

- Have you ever worried about your mentally ill loved one?

- What do you do in a crisis situation? Is there a plan?

Ideas for Between-Session Homework

- Encourage the family to learn as much as they can about their loved one's mental illness—from pamphlets, the internet, etc.

- Encourage the mentally ill parent/caregiver to attend support groups or speak with other parents who suffer from a mental illness. You may also encourage the spouse to attend available support groups as well.

- Suggest a monthly one-on-one time between the mentally ill parent/caregiver (at times when symptoms are less severe) and their child.

- If a family stressor is the stigma that a child is experiencing at school, refer the family to a local advocacy group that can assist them in obtaining support.

- If parenting is an issue, suggest that the mentally ill parent/caregiver attend a parenting class. Encourage his/her spouse to attend as well for support.

Therapeutic Activities

Activities included in this section are adapted from evidence-based practices tailored to be utilized with families with a mentally ill parent. Not all activities will apply to every family. Counselors should select those activities that best address a specific family's problem(s).

POTATO HEAD FAMILY

PARTICIPANTS

Parent/caregiver(s) and children (ages 4–15)

PURPOSE

To improve cohesion and playfulness

MATERIALS

- Raw potatoes (one per family member)
- Toothpicks
- Raisins
- Pieces of carrot
- (Other items that can be used as body parts/facial features)

DESCRIPTION

Explain to family members that life can become so chaotic at times that we forget to have fun together. Provide each family member with a raw potato, instructing them to make an image of her/himself with the raw potato adding arms, legs, facial features, etc. with toothpicks. Once family members have completed their Potato People, instruct them to have a "puppet show" depicting a fun time from the past when the mentally ill parent was present. (If the mentally ill parent is not present in the session, ask the first family member to complete her/his own Potato Person to create one of the mentally ill parent. During the "puppet show" ask the family members to take turns playing the role of the mentally ill parent.)

DISCUSSION QUESTIONS

- Whose Potato Person looks most like them?
- What was it like remembering the happy time together in the "puppet show?" What other happy memories do you have?

- Was everyone actively participating in the "puppet show?"

- What are some things that you do as a family now that are fun?

- What are some activities that you would like to do?

- What prevents you from doing more fun things together? How can you get past them?

ROLLING EMPATHY

PARTICIPANTS
Spouse/significant other and children (ages 7–18)

PURPOSE
To increase empathy and understanding

MATERIALS

- One dice

DESCRIPTION
Explain to family members that sometimes it can be frustrating watching a family member who suffers from a mental illness. It's easy to blame the person for their behavior rather than the illness itself; it's harder to have empathy for their situation. Instruct family members to take turns rolling a dice. For each roll the family member should respond/discuss the following:

- roll a one or four: talk about a time you shared a feeling (happy, sad, excited, scared, etc.) with the mentally ill family member

- roll a two or five: describe some part of what life is like for your mentally ill family member (thoughts, feelings, work, relationships, etc.)

- roll a three or six: name a way you and the mentally ill family member are alike.

DISCUSSION QUESTIONS

- What was it like discussing your mentally ill loved one in this positive way?

- Can you think of a time when you may have responded to your mentally ill loved one in a way that you regret? What did you do when this happened?

- What do you know about your loved one's mental illness?

- Was there an answer from another family member that made you rethink how you feel or treat your mentally ill loved one?

- Empathy means putting yourself in someone else's shoes. What do you think it would be like to live every day with a mental illness?

- What can you tell yourself when you find yourself being critical of your loved one with a mental illness?

DRAW IT OUT

PARTICIPANTS
Parent/caregiver(s) and children (ages 4–15)

PURPOSE
To express feelings and provide psychoeducation regarding mental illness

MATERIALS

- Paper
- Crayons or markers

DESCRIPTION
Ask family members what they know about their loved one's mental illness. Explain that there are perceptions of mental illness and that not all of them are true. Provide each family member with a piece of paper and instruct them to draw what they think their loved one's mental illness might look like. When everyone has completed their pictures ask family members to share their pictures. Use the time to correct any misperceptions and educate the family regarding their loved one's particular mental illness.

DISCUSSION QUESTIONS

- How were your pictures the same or different? What do you think this means?
- What did you learn today about your loved one's illness?
- Did you discover anything that you were wrong about? What was it like to discover something different?
- Do you have any questions that you would like to ask?
- How do you think having a better understanding of your loved one's mental illness will help you? How will it help others in your family?

WHOSE ROLE?

PARTICIPANTS
Parent/caregiver(s) and children (ages 7–18)

PURPOSE
To identify roles within the family and to establish boundaries

MATERIALS

- Index cards
- Dark colored marker

DESCRIPTION

Prior to the family's arrival, write the following roles on separate index cards (include other roles that you have identified within the family).

- The Worrier
- The Planner
- The Hater
- The Excuse-Maker
- The King
- The Complainer
- The Quiet One
- The Loud One
- The Ignorer
- The Housekeeper
- The Fighter
- The Talker
- The Boss
- The Nurturer
- The Mediator
- The Hidden One (note: If you think any roles would not pertain to the family, exclude them from this activity).

Explain to family members that people often have roles within their families. Explain that some roles can be held by more than one person; some roles are exclusively one person's; some roles are not the roles people want, etc. Place the index cards in a stack in the middle of the table and have each family member take turns drawing and reading a card. For each role that the family member reads, s/he will state what the role definition means to her/him, and which family member they think best fits that role. Family members should continue taking turns until all the roles have been read.

DISCUSSION QUESTIONS

- Is there a role that you have that you would like to "resign" from?
- Did each family member have an identified role? Would they be in these same roles if your loved one did not have a mental illness?

- Was there a role that was held by several family members? What role was it? Have there been any role changes in the home?

- If you could pick a role, which would it be?

- Is there anyone that you feel does an especially good job in her/his role? Why?

CHANGING BEHAVIOR

PARTICIPANTS
Parent/caregiver(s) and children (ages 4–15)

PURPOSE
To reduce impulsive behaviors and practice stopping and thinking

MATERIALS

- Paper or construction paper

- Scissors

- Glue or tape

- Crayons or markers

DESCRIPTION
Explain to the family that an impulsive behavior is doing something without thinking of the consequences. Often, especially when faced with conflict, individuals can act impulsively. Instruct them to make a remote control that will assist them in reminding each other to stop and think. Tell family members that they will make each button one at a time, after you have explained the function of each one. Explain the buttons described below and get the family to create the button to add to their remote.

- "Pause"—the button can be used to "pause" a child's behavior when they are "out of control" in order to give time to decide what his/her next step will be.

- "Fast Forward"—The parent/child can "fast forward" to see what the possible consequences of their actions will be.

- "Stop"—If the parent/child decides that his/her behavior will result in a negative consequence he/she can choose to stop the behavior.

- "Play"—The parent/child will continue with the original behavior.

- "Rewind"—The parent/child can "rewind" the behavior in order to think about what he/she could have done differently.

- "Volume"—To assist in recognizing when the parent/child is being too loud or needs to speak in a quieter voice; or if the parent/child is speaking so quietly that he/she is not easily heard.

- "Channel change"—The parent/child can go back through the different behaviors to select which behavior is the best choice.

Family members should then role play different impulsive scenarios that often occur in their home and the parent/caregiver(s) can practice utilizing the remote, stating out loud which button they are pushing.

DISCUSSION QUESTIONS

- Why do you think that your mother/father was given the control of the remote?

- Are their ways that you can be in charge of your own behaviors?

- In what ways can the remote help you to work on your behaviors?

- What is the hardest behavior for you to control?

- What is the hardest situation for you to control your behavior in?

- What would happen if everyone used a remote to stop and think before they do something?

HIDE AND SEEK

PARTICIPANTS
Parent/caregiver(s) and children (ages 4–17)

PURPOSE
To assist in expressing difficult feelings

MATERIALS

- Index cards

- Dark colored marker

- Tape

DESCRIPTION
Prior to the session, write various feelings words on index cards (happy, sad, anxious, jealous, brave, guilty, excited, etc.). Take the cards and tape them in various places around the room, "hiding" them— if there are younger children in the family, make sure you put some cards where they will be easy to find. Explain to family members that it can be difficult to share feelings, especially if one feels that it would be burdensome to other family members because things are "hard enough." Tell the family that you have hidden various feelings cards around the room. Taking turns, each family member should attempt to find a feelings card. Once they have found one, they should share a time they have had that feeling.

DISCUSSION QUESTIONS

- What was the easiest feeling to discuss? What was the hardest?

- Can you think of a time that you felt that you had to hide your feelings?

- Do you think that it is better or worse to hide your feelings?

- Can you think of one person in your family that you don't have to hide your feelings from?

- Can you think of a person outside of your family that you don't have to hide your feelings from?

- How did you feel listening to others' responses?

MY WORRY BOX

PARTICIPANTS
Child/ren (ages 5–18)

PURPOSE
To decrease worry

MATERIALS

- Shoebox (or another box of a similar size)

- Tape

- Paper

- Scissors

- Magazines

- Crayons or markers

- Construction paper

DESCRIPTION
Discuss with the child how sometimes we can worry so much that it affects our day. Explain that it is okay to worry, but we want to make sure that we don't worry so much that we can't do anything else. Provide the child with a shoebox and explain that s/he will be making a "worry" box. Allow the child to decorate the box however s/he would like. Then on separate pieces of paper, have the child write down all the things that s/he worries about and put them in the box. Explain that the box can be left in your office or taken home. Then suggest that a certain amount of time can be allotted for worrying each week with the worry box (compartmentalizing the problem). During that time, worries will be pulled out of the box, worried about, and then the child can decide whether that worry item needs to stay in the box or can be thrown away. Explain that s/he is only to worry during the worry time.

DISCUSSION QUESTIONS

- How often do you worry about the things in the worry box now?

- How much time do you think you should spend worrying?

- How is worrying bad for you? In what ways is it bad?

- Is there anything you put in the box that you think might not be something to worry about?

- Who can you talk to about the things that worry you?

- How can you calm yourself if you start to worry when it's not a worry time?

WHAT I CAN COUNT ON AND WHAT I CAN'T COUNT ON

PARTICIPANTS

Parent/caregiver (*not* the identified mentally ill parent) and children (ages 5–18)

PURPOSE

To increase acceptance

MATERIALS

- Paper

- Pens or pencils

DESCRIPTION

Explain to the family that in all relationships with another person, there are things we can count on and things we can't count on. Ask family members to draw a vertical line down the middle of a piece of paper and to label the two sides "Things I can count on" and "Things I can't count on." Then ask everyone to list as many things under each column as they can think of regarding their relationship with their mentally ill loved one. Examples under "Things I can count on" might be "Tells me s/he loves me when I see her/him" or "Plays games when we're together" and under "Things I can't count on" might be "Remembering my birthday" or "Remembering to call."

DISCUSSION QUESTIONS

- How are you feeling right now? Is anyone angry about the game?

- How have you handled angry feelings in the past?

- Are there things that happen in the family that you feel you have no control over?

- How do you handle times when life feels out of control or things seem unfair?

- How can you help other family members to deal with things that are not fair?

THE SCRIPT

PARTICIPANTS
Parent/caregiver(s) and children (ages 5–18)

PURPOSE
To reduce stigma

MATERIALS

- Paper
- White board or flip chart
- Dry erase markers
- Index cards
- Pens or pencils

DESCRIPTION
Discuss with family members how difficult it can be to talk with others about a loved one's mental illness. Explain that it is certainly up to them who they choose to disclose to, but sometimes they can be caught off guard and have difficulty thinking of things to say when people ask questions. Direct family members to brainstorm questions or comments that others might say to them about their loved one's mental illness and write these down on a piece of paper. After the list has been completed, read each question out loud and encourage family members to brainstorm creative responses. Get them to take turns writing these responses on the white board (or flip chart). Encourage the family to come up with both serious and humorous responses—for example, a response of, "Don't worry, it's not contagious," is acceptable. Once complete, suggest to family members that they write down their favorite responses on index cards.

DISCUSSION QUESTIONS

- Which response did you like best?
- Do people say things about your parent that makes you angry?
- What can you do to help remember ways to respond to what people ask or say?
- Which people do you feel most comfortable sharing more information with?
- Which people do you not want to have any information?

A BAG OF COPING

PARTICIPANTS
Parent/caregiver(s) and children (ages 5–18)

PURPOSE

To increase coping skills

MATERIALS

- Bag
- Index cards
- Pens or pencils

DESCRIPTION

Explain to family members that not only are there many stressors in family life, but also in life in general. It is helpful to have a "bag" of coping skills. Explain that coping skills are things that people can do or think about that allow them to calm down during times of tension (i.e. think of a peaceful place, squeeze a soft ball, breathe deeply and slowly, etc). Direct family members to take turns naming coping skills. After each person has named one, have her/him write it down on an index card and place it in the bag. When everyone has exhausted their ideas for coping skills, reread the index cards that are in the bag and have everyone suggest actual items that they could place in the bag to keep handy at home during stressful times (i.e. a picture book of beautiful places, a stress ball, bubbles, etc.). There may be coping skills where an actual item cannot be placed in the bag (i.e. take a walk). In those cases, encourage the family to simply leave the index card in the bag. Give the family the bag at the end of the session and encourage them to place some of the actual items in the bag when they are at home.

DISCUSSION QUESTIONS

- Which of the coping skills that you named have you already used? Which ones were new to you?
- Which ones do you think would work best for you when you are really stressed?
- Do the same coping skills work for everyone? Why or why not?
- How do you know if a coping skill is working?
- If one coping skill doesn't work, does that mean that none of them will work?
- What successful coping skills have you seen other family members use?

Additional Activities That May be Helpful

- It Takes a Village in Chapter 3: Single-Parent Families with an Absent Parent (p.27)
- Gaining Perspective in Chapter 6: Families with Grandparents as Caregivers (p.74)
- The Weight of Shameful Thoughts in Chapter 7: Families with an Incarcerated Loved One (p.90)

- Support in Chapter 7: Families with an Incarcerated Loved One (p.85)
- Difficult Feelings in Chapter 9: Families with Parent Substance Abuse (p.126)

References

American Academy of Children and Adolescent Psychiatry (2008) *Facts for Families: Children of Parents with Mental Illness.* Washington, DC: American Academy of Children and Adolescent Psychiatry. Available at www.aacap.org/App_Themes/AACAP/docs/facts_for_families/39_children_of_parents_with_mental_illness.pdf, accessed 5 October 2013.

Barrowclough, C. and Hooley, J.M. (2003) "Attributions and expressed emotions: a review." *Clinical Psychology Review 23,* 849–880.

Bos, A.E.R., Pryor, J.B., Reeder, G.D. and Stutterheim, S.E. (2013) "Stigma: advances in theory and research." *Basic and Applied Social Psychology 35,* 1–9.

Byrne, P. (2000) "Stigma of mental illness and ways of diminishing it." *Advances in Psychiatric Treatment 6,* 65–72.

Caton, C.L.M., Shrout, P.E., Eagle, P.F., Opler, L.A., Felix, A. and Dominguez, B. (1994) "Risk factors for homelessness among schizophrenic men: a case control study." *American Journal of Public Health 84,* 265–270.

Cavaiola, A.A. (2000) "In search of a new metaphor for the impact of drug abuse on families." *Family Therapy 27,* 2, 81–87.

Cherromas, W.M., Clarke, D. and Marchinko, S. (2008) "Relationship-based support for women living with serious mental illness." *Issues in Mental Health Nursing 29,* 437–453.

Clarke, L.A. and Annunziata, J. (2006) *Wishing Wellness: A Workbook for Children of Parents with Mental Illness.* Washington, DC: Magination Press.

De Leon, G., Sacks, S. and Wexler, H.K. (2002) "Modified Prison Therapeutic Communities for the Dual- and Multiple-Diagnosed Offender." In C.G. Leukefeld and F. Tims (eds) *Treatment of Drug Offenders: Policies and Issues.* New York: Springer.

Fadden, G., Bebbington, P. and Kuipers, L. (1987) "The burden of care: the impact of functional psychiatric illness on the patient's family." *British Journal of Psychiatry 150,* 285–292.

Heru, A.M. (2000) "Family functioning, burden, and reward in the caregiving for chronic mental illness." *Families, Systems and Health 18,* 1, 91–103.

Kessler, R.C., Berglund, P.A., Bruce, M.L., Koch, J.R., Laska, E.M., Leaf, P.J., Manderscheid, R.W., Rosenheck, R.A., Walters, E.E. and Wang, P.S. (2001) "The prevalence and correlates of untreated serious mental illness." *Health Services Research 36,* 987–1007.

Kessler, R.C., Chiu, W.T., Demler, O. and Walters, E.E. (2005) "Prevalence, severity, and comorbidity of 12-month *DSM-IV* disorders in the national comorbidity survey replication." *Archives of General Psychiatry 62,* 617–709.

Kessler, R.C., McGonagle, K.A., Zhao, S., Nelson, C.B., Hughes, M., Eshleman, S., Wittchen, H.U. and Kendler, K.S. (1994) "Lifetime and 12-month prevalence of *DSM-III-R* psychiatric disorders in the United States." *Archives of General Psychiatry 51,* 8–19.

Miklowitz, D.J. (2007) "The role of the family in the course and treatment of bipolar disorder." *Association for Psychological Science 16,* 192–196.

Miklowitz, D., Otto, M., Frank, E., Reily Harrington, N., Wisniewski, S., Kogan, J., Nierenberg, A., Calabrese, R., Marangell, L., Gyulai, L., Araga, M., Gonzalez, J., Shirley, E., Thase, M. and Sachs, G. (2007) "Psychosocial treatments for bipolar depression: a 1-year randomized trial from the Systematic Treatment Enhancement Program." *Archives of General Psychiatry 64,* 419–427.

Miller, I., Keitner, G., Ryan, C., Solomon, D. and Cardemil, E. (2005) "Treatment matching in the posthospital care of depressed inpatients." *American Journal of Psychiatry 162,* 2131– 2138.

National Alliance on Mental Health (2013a) *Mental Illnesses.* Arlington, VA: National Alliance on Mental Health. Available at www.nami.org/Template.cfm?Section=By_Illness, accessed 5 October 2013.

National Alliance on Mental Health (2013b) *Mental Illnesses*. Arlington, VA: National Alliance on Mental Health. Available at www.nami.org/factsheets/mentalillness_factsheet.pdf, accessed 5 October 2013.

Pfammatter, M., Junghan, U. and Brenner, H. (2006) "Efficacy of psychological therapy in schizophrenia: conclusions from meta-analyses." *Schizophrenia Bulletin 32*, 1, 64–80.

Rea, M., Tompson, M., Miklowitz, D., Goldstein, M., Hwang, S. and Mintz, J. (2003) "Family-focused treatment versus individual treatment for bipolar disorders and suicide disorder: results of a randomized clinical trial." *Journal of Consulting and Clinical Psychology 7*, 482–492.

Regier, D.A., Boyd, J.H., Burke, J.D. Jr., Rae, D.S., Myers, J.K., Kramer, M., Robins, L.N., George, L.K., Karno, M. and Locke, B.Z. (1988) "One month prevalence of mental disorders in the United States." *Archives of General Psychiatry 45*, 977–986.

Schock-Giordano, A.M. and Gavazzi, S.M. (2005) "Mental Illness and Family Stress." In P.C McKenry and S.J. Price (eds) *Families and Change: Coping with Stressful Events and Transitions* (3rd edition). Thousand Oaks: Sage Publications.

Swofford, C., Kasckow, J., Scheller-Gilkey, G. and Inderbitzin, L.B. (1996) "Substance use: a powerful predictor of relapse in schizophrenia." *Schizophrenia Research 20*, 145–151.

CHAPTER 11

Families with a Chronically Ill Child

Introduction

All children have various illnesses during childhood, but most children recover from these quickly and there is no interference with daily life and development. For approximately 20 percent of school-age children, however, *chronic health conditions* impair daily functioning throughout their childhoods (Kliewer 1997). Goodman (2001) defines a chronic illness as:

> a disorder with a protracted course that can be fatal or associated with a relatively normal life span despite impaired physical or mental functioning. Chronic illness or disease differs from acute illness in that (1) it is treatable yet not curable, thus needs management for long periods of time, and therefore, (2) the responsibility for the management of the illness is shared and/or transferred to the child and family.

Examples of chronic medical conditions include:

- asthma (most common)
- diabetes
- cerebral palsy
- sickle cell anemia
- cystic fibrosis
- epilepsy
- spina bifida
- congenital heart problems
- juvenile rheumatoid arthritis
- hemophilia
- cancer
- AIDS.

Although chronic medical conditions include very different illnesses and treatments, children and families dealing with these illnesses have much in common. The individual and family stresses and resiliencies are often very similar.

Vulnerabilities

The diagnosis of a chronic disease in childhood can challenge family balance and can affect every family member with anger, grief and increased interpersonal stress (Pradeep, Pradhan and Shah 2004). The child her/himself often is fearful of the illness and of painful treatments. Hospital stays can be scary and lonely. Children's activity can be limited and, over time, they can become more and more aware of their family's sacrifices and stress. These phenomena have the potential to cause chronically ill children to feel negatively about themselves. Indeed, in a meta-analysis of 621 studies, Pinquart (2013) found that children with chronic illnesses have lower self-esteem than their healthier peers.

There is also significant stress for parents. Research shows that parents of chronically ill children are at risk of psychological disorders and poorer physical health outcomes than parents of healthy children (Cohen 1999). Handling the physical, medical and emotional needs of a chronically ill child certainly takes its toll. Many parents are no longer able to engage in their own personal interests and hobbies while other parents report grieving the loss of their pre-child relationship (Fidika, Salewski and Goldbeck 2013; Peck and Lillibridge 2003). In fact, caring for children with chronic conditions puts such high demands on parents that the experience can be much like a traumatic event (Horsch *et al.* 2007; Lord, Wastell and Ungerer 2005).

Parents also describe experiencing difficulties in setting limits for their chronically ill child (Uzark and Jones 2003). They become more lenient out of guilt or sympathy for the child's medical limitations and no longer enforce family rules. Parents can also become so overwhelmed with medical care that they can overlook their child's normal developmental needs (Sullivan-Bolyai *et al.* 2003).

Siblings of chronically ill children are also at risk of experiencing mental health problems and psychosocial adjustment (Besier *et al.* 2010; Sharpe and Rossiter 2002). Studies show that they are at increased risk of depression, anxiety, guilt, peer problems, academic problems, symptoms of post-traumatic stress and perceptions of poor quality of life (Cadman, Boyle and Offord 1988; Cohen, Friedrich and Jaworski 1994; Houtzager *et al.* 2004; Pynoos *et al.* 1987). Siblings are exposed to the physical and emotional pain of their sibling's illness and fear, along with their parents' distress and extended separations from the ill sibling and the parents because of hospitalizations. Sibling relationships are important because sibling conflict in families with chronically ill children can cause lower self-esteem and weaker general family cohesion, and the ill child can experience more difficulties adjusting to her/his medical regimen (Hanson *et al.* 1992).

Strengths

In resilient families with a chronically ill child, there is greater flexibility, attachment and cohesion among family members (Lee *et al.* 2004). These families seem to use illness as another way to pull together and support one another. They are able to change their structure in order to solve problems when stressors are encountered.

While having a brother or sister with a chronic illness is indeed a risk factor for psychological problems, many siblings do adjust well. Some studies even show valuable effects such as social maturity and prosocial behavior (Horwitz and Kazak 1990). This suggests that many siblings can use the adversity of their sister or brother's illness to develop empathy, social competence, self-help skills and adaptive behavior.

Empirical Support for Potential Treatment Approaches

Family work is often included in working with chronic illness, as family members can have a positive effect on illness management. Family work is helpful for ventilation of feelings and clarification of misinformation. Turmoil in the family can stress and weaken immune systems and lead to increased risk of symptom exacerbation (Schmidt and Schmidt 1991).

Fidika *et al.* (2013) found that increased levels of perceived social support were associated with parents' quality of life when caring for a chronically ill child. This finding suggests that caregiving stress is buffered by a robust social support system. Social support systems can be emotional (i.e. sympathy and nurturance), tangible (i.e. caregiving and financial assistance), informational (i.e. advice and data) and companionship (i.e. sense of belonging and connection).

In an intensive form of Behavioral Family Systems Therapy (BFST), which used problem-solving, communication skills training and cognitive restructuring, significant improvements were seen in youth treatment adherence, blood sugar levels and diabetes-related family conflict, even at 12-month follow-up (Wysocki *et al.* 2007). In a meta-analysis of 26 studies of various child illnesses, cognitive behavioral therapies (CBT) significantly improved child symptoms, while problem-solving therapy significantly improved parent mental health (Trivedi 2013).

For siblings, Sidhu, Passmore and Baker (2006) found improved mental health after a four-day camp intervention for healthy siblings of pediatric cancer patients. The program focused on age-appropriate information about the disease, social skills and stress management. Besier *et al.* (2010) point to the importance of allowing siblings to talk about their own perceptions and to be able to express such feelings as resentment and anger. They recommend specific parent–child sessions in order to strengthen the often neglected relationship.

Resources

- *How Parents Can Help Children Cope with a Chronic Illness*: http://dbafoundation. org/wp-content/uploads/2012/11/4ChronicIllnessInsert.pdf

- American Academy of Pediatrics, *Siblings with Chronic Illness*: http://www. healthychildren.org/English/health-issues/conditions/chronic/Pages/ Siblings-of-Children-with-Chronic-Ilnesses.aspx

- *Welcome to Holland*: www.our-kids.org/Archives/Holland.html

- Brave Kids: www.bravekids.org

- PBS's Arthur's *Hooray for Health*: www.pbs.org/parents/arthur/lesson/ health/

- Educational advocacy for patients with chronic illness: www. thejenniferjaffcenter.org

Counselor Cautions

Several of the activities in this chapter do not require the entire family. It is important that counselors discuss this with the parent/caregiver(s) in advance. Particularly when parent/caregiver(s) attend alone, counselors should be sensitive to childcare challenges and should attempt to schedule sessions at convenient times for the family. Even when the entire family is attending a session, the counselor should be sensitive to scheduling, as there may be other medical appointments that the family is trying to juggle.

Because these families may be involved in several different "systems" (i.e., school, medical, counseling, etc.) collaboration may be important. Counselors should ask families if they would like this collaboration and obtain the appropriate consents and releases of information.

Discussion Questions

- What are your family's strengths as a whole? What are some of each individual's strengths?

- What does your family do for fun? What obstacles are there to having more fun times together? How can you overcome these?

- How has *<illness>* impacted your child's life?

- How has *<illness>* impacted your family life?

- How do you manage stress during stressful times?

- What are healthy ways to express any anger that you're feeling about the *<illness>*?

- What friends or extended family members can all of you count on?

- What are some ways to encourage each other when you notice that someone is feeling down?

Ideas for Between-Session Homework

- Encourage parent/caregiver(s) to attend support groups or speak with other parents whose child is successfully managing the same diagnosis.

- Assign parent/caregiver(s) a date night.

- Suggest a monthly one-on-one time between a parent/caregiver and a sibling.

- If one of the parent/caregiver(s) stresses is school, refer them to a local advocacy group that can assist them in obtaining accommodations through disability legislation.

Therapeutic Activities

Activities included in this section are experiential opportunities to address typical but specific family issues related to families with a chronically ill child. Not all activities will apply to every family. Counselors should select those activities that best address a specific family's problem(s).

NO MORE STINKIN' THINKIN'

PARTICIPANTS
Parent/caregiver(s) only

PURPOSE
To reduce parent stress

MATERIALS

- Paper
- Pens/pencils

DESCRIPTION
Explain to the parent/caregiver(s) that stress is caused not just by a stressful event itself, but also by the way we *think about* the event. Consequently, parents' *perceptions* about the stress caused by their child's illness affect their own psychological adjustment. Ask parent/caregiver(s) to draw a vertical line down the middle of a piece of paper. Then ask them to think about times when they have been particularly stressed about their chronically ill child and to remember what it was that they were *thinking* at the time. Ask them to write down those thoughts on the left-hand side of the paper, along with any other negative thoughts that they have experienced about their child's situation or their abilities to cope. (Examples might be, "My child is never going to be able to live away from home" or "I'm not going to be able to do this.") Then ask them to read each thought one by one while the counselor challenges it, using some of the following questions.

- Is that thought accurate? Is it logical?
- What objective evidence/facts are there to support this thought?
- What alternative views are there about the situation?
- Are you underestimating your ability to cope?
- Does your thought help you accomplish your goals?
- What is the worst that can happen if your thought is correct?
- What is the worst thing that could happen to your or your family and how does this situation compare to that?

Afterwards ask the parent/caregiver to rewrite her/his original thought on the right-hand side of the page so that it is more accurate and less distorted. Continue to examine negative thoughts (stinkin' thinkin'!) with corrective thoughts written beside each.

DISCUSSION QUESTIONS

- What are your thoughts about this exercise?
- Do you agree that the way we *think* about a situation can either make things harder or easier?
- How hard will it be for you to change some of your negative thoughts? Which one will be the *most* difficult?
- What are some ways you can catch yourself when you are starting to engage in stinkin' thinkin'?
- How can you help each other change your stinkin' thinkin' without making each other angry?
- Are there thoughts that you feel are impossible to change? What are they?
- Are there specific times where you feel you are more vulnerable to stinkin' thinkin'?
- Does your stinkin' thinkin' affect others in the family?

SUPPORT

PARTICIPANTS
Parent/caregiver(s) only

PURPOSE
To recognize existing and potential supports

MATERIALS

- Dry marker board or flip chart paper
- Dry erase markers

DESCRIPTION

Explain to the parent/caregiver(s) that social support is critical to their mental health and to their family's quality of life. Explain that there are different types of social support and that you will be identifying existing supports and brainstorming potential supports. Then make four columns on your dry marker board or flip chart paper. Label these "Emotional Support," "Esteem Support," "Information Support" and "Tangible Support." If needed, the following explanations can be given for each kind of support.

- Emotional support: people, groups and places that express care and concern, such as "I'm so sorry that you are having to go through this."

- Esteem support: people, groups and places that express beliefs in a parent/caregiver(s)'s ability to handle a problem, such as "You are such a good problem-solver."

- Information support: people, groups and places that provide useful information, such as "I'll get the information on the pharmaceutical company's Patient Assistance Program for you."

- Tangible support: people, groups and places that can provide physical assistance, such as making a meal, providing respite care, financial assistance etc.

Ask the parent/caregiver(s) to begin naming people, groups and places where they already receive these types of supports. Write these down in the appropriate columns. Then brainstorm with them potential people, groups and places and write these in the appropriate columns.

DISCUSSION QUESTIONS

- Which area of social support has been easiest for you to obtain and which has been the most difficult for you to obtain?

- Which area of social support do you need most right now?

- What percentage of your social support comes from extended family, from friends and from agencies? Does this seem about right to you?

- How willing are you to *ask* for support from these people, groups and places?

- Have there been times when you needed support but you weren't able to ask for it? Why?

- Have you ever been a support for someone else? How did it make you feel to be able to provide support?

- Of the *potential* social support people, groups and places that you identified, which one do you think you will contact first?

WE DESERVE MEDALS

PARTICIPANTS
Parent/caregiver(s) and children (ages 5–18)

PURPOSE
To enhance cohesion and build self-esteem

MATERIALS

- Jar lids
- Ribbon
- Aluminum foil
- Markers
- Colored construction paper
- Scissors
- Glue

DESCRIPTION
Explain to the family that during stressful times families often forget to acknowledge one another's talents and strengths. Describe how important it is for families to praise and acknowledge one another. Then lay out all of the craft supplies and instruct each family member to create a medal for the person on her/his left. Remind everyone to be sure to write the name of the award on it (Best Speller, Good Sport, #1 Helper, Greatest Joke Teller etc.). When everyone has completed their medal, invite the family to have an Awards Ceremony where they award each other the medals they have made.

DISCUSSION QUESTIONS

- What was it like to make and award your family member a medal?
- What was it like to *receive* a medal from a family member?
- Did you agree with the medal that you received?
- What do you think your medal says about you?
- What other medals do you think should be given to each of your family members?
- What medals do you think should be given to people *outside* of your family?
- What will you do with your medal?

STORYTELLING GONE WILD

PARTICIPANTS
One parent/caregiver and one sibling (ages 5–11)

PURPOSE

To give special attention to siblings

MATERIALS

- None

DESCRIPTION

Explain to the parent and sibling that laughter is affiliative—in other words, it helps people feel closer and more connected. Sharing fun times with a parent is very important for siblings of chronically ill children. Explain that you will be giving them a "story starter" and that they should take turns adding one or two sentences to the story, making it as silly as they can. Allow two to three minutes for each story and then start another one. Here are some examples of "story starters."

- "Once upon a time Cinderella met the Big Bad Wolf…"

- "The three little pigs decided to build a storm shelter…"

- "The seven dwarfs decided to leave the country and head for New York City…"

- "There was once a mouse and a cat who were best friends…"

- "Once upon a time there was an elephant who hated peanuts…"

DISCUSSION QUESTIONS

- Which was your favorite story? Why?

- How do you think the two of you worked together as a story-writing team?

- How would you describe each of your laughs?

- What memories do you have of laughing together as a family?

- What are some funny things that your family could do together?

- Do you think that laughing together is good for you? Why?

TALK TO IT!

PARTICIPANTS

Chronically ill child and siblings (ages 6–18) only

PURPOSE

To enhance communication/understanding and reduce blame

MATERIALS

- Paper

- Crayons/markers

DESCRIPTION

Explain to the children that the ill child is not the problem—the disease is the problem. Then invite each of them to draw their own picture of what they think the disease itself would look like if it had a form. After everyone has completed their pictures invite each child to talk to their picture as if it were the disease itself. Encourage them to name the ways it has hurt each one of them and the ways it has helped each one of them be stronger.

DISCUSSION QUESTIONS

- What were the similarities and differences in your pictures?
- How are your *thoughts and feelings* toward the disease similar and different?
- What did you learn about each other from this exercise?
- What did you learn about the disease from this exercise?
- Is there anything you want to talk to your parents about after doing this exercise?
- What do you want to do with your pictures?

BOARD GAME FOR ILLNESS IN THE FAMILY

PARTICIPANTS

Parent/caregiver and children (ages 6 and up)

PURPOSE

To improve communication and cohesion

MATERIALS

- Snakes and Ladders board game
- Appendix A cards (discussion, interactions and feelings)
- Appendix I cards (illness)

DESCRIPTION

Make photocopies of the four sets of game cards (Appendices A and I) using four different colors of copy paper (or simply write "Illness," "Discussion," "Interactions" and "Feelings" on the backs of the appropriate cards). Then play Snakes and Ladders (moving up or down the board if you land on a ladder or a snake) with a difference—when players land on a numbered space they must answer a question from one of the four sets of cards. If they land on numbers 1–25 they should answer an "Illness" card; if they land on numbers 26–50 they should answer a "Discussion" card; if they land on numbers 51–75 they should answer an "Interactions" card; if they land on numbers 76–100 they should answer a "Feelings" card. The first player to reach the top wins.

DISCUSSION QUESTIONS

- What was it like to play a game together?

- What did you learn about one another?

- Were there any difficult questions to answer?

- What parts did you like best in the game?

- Who shared most easily and who had a hard time sharing?

- What will you "take away" from this game in terms of things you'd like to do differently?

STRESSES, STRESSES = SOLUTIONS, SOLUTIONS

PARTICIPANTS
Parent/caregiver and children (ages 7 and up)

PURPOSE
To improve communication and cohesion

MATERIALS

- Index cards

- Pens/pencils

- Dice (enough so that all family members have one)

DESCRIPTION
Explain to the family that stresses are problems that can be solved if several solutions are generated to pick from. Hand each family member three index cards and a pen or pencil. Ask them to write down, on separate cards, what stresses them in each of the following places: at home, at work/school and in the community (restaurants, banks, doctors', offices, etc.). When everyone has finished writing, collect the cards, mix them up and place them in a stack face down in the middle of the table. Then give everyone a dice and ask them all to roll at the same time. The highest number draws a card (if there is a tie with the highest number, the two people with the high numbers roll again), reads the stressor (or problem) and gives three solutions for it. Repeat until all of the cards have been answered.

DISCUSSION QUESTIONS

- Why is coming up with several solutions to a problem a good idea?

- What was it like to hear your stressor read out and solved by other family members?

- How easy or difficult was it for you to come up with solutions?

- Are there ever problems that don't have solutions? What do you do then?
- Do you think you'll use any of the solutions that were mentioned during the activity?
- What did you learn about problem-solving from doing this activity?

FAMILY MISSION STATEMENT

PARTICIPANTS
Parent/caregiver(s) and children (ages 7 and up)

PURPOSE
To enhance cohesion and cooperation

MATERIALS

- Piece of butcher paper or poster board
- Markers or crayons

DESCRIPTION
Explain to the family that discussing shared values and goals enhances family cohesiveness. Then direct the family to discuss and finalize a Family Mission Statement—a combined, agreed-upon manifestation of what their family is all about. A Family Mission Statement captures, in a few succinct sentences, the essence of the family's purpose. Coming up with a statement that everyone agrees upon may take quite a bit of time. Once it is decided upon, ask the family to create (and decorate) a banner with their Family Mission Statement on it together.

DISCUSSION QUESTIONS

- Does everyone agree with the Family Mission Statement that you came up with?
- How difficult was it to decide what your Family Mission Statement would be?
- What do you think your Family Mission Statement says about you as a family?
- Does your Family Mission Statement inspire you in any way?
- What can you do to remind yourselves of this Family Mission Statement through the next weeks, months and years?

ROCKING WITH PEACE

PARTICIPANTS
Parent/caregiver(s) and children (ages 5 and up)

PURPOSE

To improve stress management

MATERIALS

- Smooth small- to medium-size rocks
- Paints
- Paintbrushes

DESCRIPTION

Explain to the family that during stressful times it can be helpful to quiet the mind and think peaceful thoughts. Give each family member a rock and ask them to each select a word from the following list:

- peace
- acceptance
- joy
- love
- gratitude
- calm
- harmony
- tranquility
- harmony
- relaxation
- tenderness
- thankfulness
- serenity.

Then ask them to decorate their rock with the word they have chosen and any kind of design that seems to fit it. After the rocks have been painted and dried, encourage the family to place all of them together in an open container (i.e. basket, bowl, etc.) in the house so that they are easily visible. Suggest to the family that during stressful times it may be helpful to purposely look at the rocks, handle them and think about the words on them.

DISCUSSION QUESTIONS

- How did you decide which words you wanted?
- How do all of your words fit together? Are there any themes or is it a nice variety?
- How does thinking about these words help reduce stress?

- Where can you place these rocks in your home so that you can easily see them each day?

SIBLING LIKENESSES AND DIFFERENCES

PARTICIPANTS
Chronically ill child and one sibling* (ages 7 and up)
*This exercise can be repeated with other siblings

PURPOSE
To identify sibling commonalities and accept differences

MATERIALS

- Large piece of paper or poster board
- Pens or pencils

DESCRIPTION
Explain to the family that empathy and cohesion are increased when commonalities are identified. And, while no two people are exactly alike, those commonalities can bring them together. By the same token, accepting and embracing differences can decrease conflict. Draw a Venn diagram on a large piece of paper or poster board.

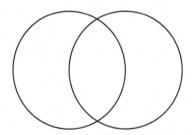

Ask one child to write qualities about her/himself that are different from the sibling on the left side of the left circle and the other child to write qualities about her/himself that are different from the first sibling on the right side of the right circle. Then let them take turns writing their common characteristics in the middle (where the circles overlap). Categories that they can consider are looks, talents, hobbies, health issues, favorite subjects, favorite movies/TV shows, favorite songs, etc.

DISCUSSION QUESTIONS

- What things do the two of you have in common? Did you realize that there were so many things?
- What does it feel like to know that you are similar in those ways?

- How are you different? What are some of the things that you like about the other one's differences?

- How are both of you similar and different from your parents or other brothers and sisters?

- How did you like working together on this project?

- Are there other things that you do together just the two of you?

Additional Activities That May be Helpful

- It Takes a Village in Chapter 3: Single-Parent Families with an Absent Parent (p.27)

- Family Shield in Chapter 3: Single-Parent Families with an Absent Parent (p.28)

- My Superhero Cape in Chapter 4: Divorced/Separated/Unmarried Families—Both parents available (p.45)

- A Strand of Angels in Chapter 9: Families with Parent Substance Abuse (p.125)

- My Worry Box in Chapter 10: Families with a Mentally Ill Parent (p.146)

- A Bag of Coping in Chapter 10: Families with a Mentally Ill Parent (p.148)

References

Besier, T., Hölling, H., Schlack, R., West, C. and Goldbeck, L. (2010) "Impact of a family-oriented rehabilitation programme on behavioural and emotional problems in healthy siblings of chronically ill children." *Child: Care, Health and Development 36*, 5, 686–695.

Cadman, D., Boyle, M. and Offord, D. (1988) "The Ontario child health study: social adjustment and mental health of siblings of children with chronic health problems." *Journal of Developmental and Behavioral Pediatrics 9*, 117–121.

Cohen, M.S. (1999) "Families coping with childhood chronic illness: a research review." *Family Systems Health 17*, 2, 149–164.

Cohen, D.S., Friedrich, W.N. and Jaworski, T. (1994) "Pediatric cancer: predicting sibling adjustment." *Journal of Clinical Psychology 50*, 303–319.

Fidika, A., Salewski, C. and Goldbeck, L. (2013) "Quality of life among parents of children with phenylketonuria (PKU)." *Health and Quality of Life Outcomes.* Available at www.hqlo.com/content/11/1/54, accessed 6 October 2013.

Goodman, R. (2001) "Children with a chronic illness: the interface of medicine and mentalhealth." *Child Study Center Newsletter 5*, 4, 1–6.

Hanson, C.L., Henggeler, S.W., Harris, M.A., Cigrang, J.A., Schinkel, A.M., Rodrigue, J.R. (1992) "Contributions of sibling relations to the adaptation of youths with insulin-dependent diabetes mellitus." *Journal of Consulting and Clinical Psychology 60*, 104–112.

Horsch, A., McManus, F., Kennedy, P. and Edge, J. (2007) "Anxiety, depressive, and posttraumatic stress symptoms in mothers of children with type 1 diabetes." *Journal of Traumatic Stress 20*, 881–891.

Horwitz, W.A. and Kazak, A.E. (1990) "Family adaptation to childhood cancer: sibling and family systems variables." *Journal of Clinical Child Psychology 19*, 3, 221–228.

Houtzager, B.A., Grootenhuis, M.A., Caron, H.N. and Last, B.F (2004) "Quality of life and psychological adaptation in siblings of paediatric cancer patients, 2 years after diagnosis." *Psycho-Oncology 13*, 499–511.

Kliewer, W. (1997) "Children's Coping with Chronic Illness." In S.A. Wolchik and I.N. Sandler (eds) *Handbook of Children's Coping: Linking Theory and Intervention.* New York: Plenum Press.

Lee, I., Lee, E.O., Kim, H.S., Park, Y.S., Song, M. and Park, Y.H. (2004) "Concept development of family resilience: a study of Korean families with a chronically ill child." *Journal of Clinical Nursing 13*, 636–645.

Lord, B., Wastell, C. and Ungerer, J. (2005) "Parent reactions to childhood Phenylketonia." *Families, Systems, and Health 23*, 2, 204–219.

Peck, B. and Lillibridge, J. (2003) "Rural fathers' experience of loss in day-to-day life of chronically ill children." *Australian Journal of Advanced Nursing 21*,1, 20–27.

Pinquart, M. (2013) "Self-esteem of children and adolescents with chronic illness: a meta-analysis." *Child: Care, Health and Development 39*, 2, 153–161.

Pradeep, R., Pradhan, M. and Shah, H. (2004) "Psychopathology and coping in parents of chronically ill children." *The Indian Journal of Pediatrics 71*, 8, 695–699.

Pynoos, R., Frederick, S., Nader, K. and Arroyo, W. (1987) "Life threat and posttraumatic stress in school age children." *Archives of General Psychiatry 44*, 1057–1063.

Schmidt, D.D. and Schmidt, P.M. (1991) "Family systems, stress, and infectious diseases." *Advances 7*, 7–15.

Sharpe, D. and Rossiter, L. (2002) "Siblings of children with a chronic illness: a meta-aanalysis." *Journal of Pediatric Psychology, 27*, 8, 699–710.

Sidhu, R., Passmore, A. and Baker, D. (2006) "The effectiveness of a peer support camp for siblings of children with cancer." *Pediatric Blood and Cancer 47*, 580–588.

Sullivan-Bolyai, S., Deatrick, J., Gruppuso, W.T., Tamborlane, W. and Grey, M. (2003) "Constant vigilance: mothers' work parenting young children with type 1 diabetes." *Journal of Pediatric Nursing 18*, 21–29.

Trivedi, D. (2013) "Cochrane review summary: psychological interventions for parents of children and adolescents with chronic illness." *Primary Health Care Research and Development 14*, 3, 224–228.

Uzark, K. and Jones, K. (2003) "Parenting stress and children with heart disease." *Journal of Pediatric Health Care 17*, 163–168.

Wysocki, T., Harris, M.A., Buckloh, L.M., Mertlich, D., Lochrie, A.S., Mauras, N. and White, N.H. (2007) "Randomized trial of behavioral family systems therapy for diabetes: maintenance of effects on adolescents' diabetes outcomes." *Diabetes Care 30*, 555–560.

CHAPTER 12

Families in Grief

Introduction

There are approximately 2.4 million deaths in the United States each year, affecting eight to ten million surviving family members (Kung *et al.* 2008). Death is a family crisis and is recognized as one of the most stressful events that a family can face. While grieving is expected, family members often grieve in diverse ways and can become confused, overwhelmed and/or overprotective of one another's grieving processes. Family structure is permanently changed with the loss of an individual member and the role that s/he played in the family. This requires great amounts of adaptation on the part of the family.

Family adaptation to loss varies. It is affected by the specific characteristics of the loss. Some of these features include:

- nature of the attachment
- perceptions regarding whether the loss was natural or manmade
- degree of preventability
- degree of expectedness
- senselessness
- witnessing of the death (Doka 1996; Stroebe and Schut 2001).

In addition, the death of a loved one in a specific family position also plays a role in individual family members' adjustment. For example, the death of one's *child* is considered the toughest loss and parent reactions can indeed resemble post-traumatic stress (Znoj and Keller 2002). While high divorce rates among bereaved parents have *not* been shown in research, the level of marital satisfaction does appear to decrease during the five years after the death (Murphy 2008). The death of a *sibling* can cause a surviving sibling to try to fulfill the deceased child's roles or to act in a completely opposite manner. Siblings can also inhibit their own grief as a way to protect a parent. The death of a *spouse* can create identity and self-definition issues. And the death of a *parent* can trigger complicated grief or traumatic grief in young children and adolescents, but can also create growth (Melhem *et al.* 2007; Wolchik *et al.* 2008).

Older theories of grief suggested sequential stages, such as denial, anger, bargaining, depression and acceptance (Kubler-Ross 1973), but newer research shows that stage models are too simplistic. Bowlby (1980) noted the ebb and flow of processes such as Shock/Numbness, Yearning/Searching, Disorganization/Despair and Reorganization.

Despite its inevitability, death is a taboo subject. We deny the reality of death, we believe it should be defeated through modern medicine and technology and we have removed ourselves from witnessing death, placing dying loved ones in hospitals and other health care institutions. Euphemisms such as people are "no longer with us," have "passed away," gone "to meet their Maker," "kicked the bucket," etc. avoid clear and honest discussions, making it difficult for families to openly talk and grieve.

Potential Challenges/Vulnerabilities

Although death and grieving are normal, bereaved family members can experience physical, psychological and/or social symptoms following the death of a loved one. Bereavement can lower immune systems, aggravate existing medical conditions, interrupt sleep and increase the abuse of drugs and alcohol (Hall and Irwin 2001; Stroebe, Schut and Stroebe 2007). It can also affect social status, personal identity, role clarity and support (Rosenblatt 2000; Weiss 2008).

Mikulincer and Shaver (2008) suggest that those with an anxious-ambivalent or avoidant attachment to the deceased struggle more with chronic mourning, somatization and cognitive suppression. Shear, Boelen and Neimeyer (2011) found three groups of risk factors for pathological grief: an individual's personal psychological vulnerability, a toxic or unsupportive family system and unexpected, violent or preventable death.

Deaths due to suicide and homicide certainly can create particular challenges in grief counseling. While those family members affected by suicide struggle with shame and blame, family members affected by homicide most often develop symptoms of post-traumatic stress disorder (Webb 2004).

Strengths

Loss is often linked with personal growth or a changed sense of self-growth beyond a previous level of functioning (Tedeschi and Calhoun 2008). Indeed, many bereaved persons are changed by the grief experience in ways that create new identities and worldviews. They describe themselves as more vulnerable but also stronger and more independent. Many describe finding new insight into the meaning of life and/or a greater appreciation for relationships. Some develop an enhanced spirituality and others get involved in causes or projects that help others; still others find a new compassion in themselves as a result of their grief.

Those who emerge from their grief with personal growth do so because of positive coping (such as support seeking or positive reframing).

Empirical Support for Potential Treatment Approaches

The grief and loss literature states that the goal for grieving individuals is to integrate the bereavement experience into daily life and to "come to terms with the loss" (e.g. Barrera *et al.* 2007). Research suggests that successful adaptation to life after a loved one's death includes emotional support, problem-focused coping, meaning-making, positive religious coping and personal growth (Affeck and Tennen 1996; Linley and Joseph 2004).

Stroebe and Schut (1999) describe a dual-process bereavement model—*loss orientation coping* and *restoration orientation coping. Loss orientation* concentrates on the bereaved's grief and loss; *restoration orientation* focuses on adjusting to life after the loss (Wijngaards-de Meij *et al.* 2008). *Loss-orientation* involves a painful dwelling on, even searching for, the lost person. *Restoration-orientation* refers to the focus on reorienting oneself in a changed world without the deceased person. Caserta and Lund (2007) demonstrated that better outcomes emerge from attention to both types of coping. Stroebe and Schut (2008) suggest that *complicated grief* may indeed stem from an over-focus on only one coping orientation (and avoiding the other) or difficulty oscillating back and forth between the two.

Research also shows that adaptation is increased when individuals have good personal emotional-regulation capacities, when there is cohesion and adaptability in the family system and when there is marital intimacy (Nadeau 2008; Shapiro 2001). Gilbert (1996) maintained that the family's ability to openly communicate and accept one another's varying grief styles are the most important factors in family adaptation. She described important gender differences in grieving such as men's tendency to suffer less intense grief that resolves more quickly. Along those lines, Morgan (2000) suggests that men primarily share their grief only with their spouses, whereas women confide not only to spouses but also to a wider network of relatives and friends.

Resources

- Sesame Street: *Grief Resources and Distribution Partners*: www.sesamestreet.org/parents/topicsandactivities/toolkits/tlc/griefresources

- PBS: *When Families Grieve*: www.pbs.org/parents/whenfamiliesgrieve/resources.html

- The Compassionate Friends: www.compassionatefriends.org/home.aspx

- The Dougy Center: www.dougy.org

Counselor Cautions

Counselors should consider themselves collaborators rather than experts as they work with families in grief. Only family members know the real depth and meaning of their particular loss. They are the experts in their own grief and counselors should be cautioned not to assume that this particular family's grief work is like another's. It is often helpful for counselors to acknowledge to the family that the family members are experts on their own grief.

While family cohesion is helpful in grieving families, it is important that counselors and the family support individual family members' styles of grieving. Families often have expectations that they should share the same feelings and grief behaviors, but this is typically not the case.

While social support and spirituality are thought to have healing benefits to the bereaved, this is not always the case—both can complicate or facilitate grieving. Supporters can listen but they can also express unrealistic expectations. Believing in a higher (God's) plan can help make meaning out of loss but it can also create anger towards God. Counselors are cautioned to carefully assess each family's social support system and spiritual beliefs before assuming that these resources will be beneficial.

Discussion Questions

- How did you find out about the death of your loved one? Who told you?

- Who have you had to tell about your loved one's death? Did you want to do this or did you feel forced? What did you say?

- How has this loss affected your spirituality?

- Who is included in your emotional support group? Is there anyone in particular that you feel you can talk to more than others?

- Is there something that people say that really bugs you? How can you address it?

- Who in your family talks most easily about your deceased love one? Who talks least about her/him? What do you think this means?

- Are there any activities that you used to do with your loved one that you have stopped doing? Do you feel like you will ever be able to do that again? If so, how will you start doing this again?

- How do you want to remember your deceased loved one—to continue to hold her/him close?

Ideas for Between-Session Homework

- There are many wonderful children's books about death and grief. Ask parents to obtain some of these books and read them to their children.

- Assign couples a date night. Encourage them to do something away from other children and the responsibilities of home and work.

- Encourage families to have as many meal times together as possible. Assign them topics to discuss, such as "my success/accomplishment of the day," "best and worst experiences of the day," "who was nice to me today and what s/he did," etc.

- Recommend specific support groups if needed. Many hospice programs and funeral homes have bereavement support groups and there are specialized support groups such as Compassionate Friends for grieving parents and siblings. Each community will have its own resources.

- If the family is close to the anniversary of their loved one's death, have them make a plan for the date—decide ways to commemorate the anniversary.

Therapeutic Activities

Activities included in this section are experiential opportunities to address typical but specific family issues related to family bereavement. It is not expected that all activities will apply to all families. Counselors should select those activities that best address a specific family's problem(s).

QUESTIONS, QUESTIONS, QUESTIONS

PARTICIPANTS
Parent/caregiver(s) and children (ages 4–18)

PURPOSE
To clearly understand the circumstances around the loved one's death and to make meaning of the loss

MATERIALS

- None

DESCRIPTION
Prior to the exercise, meet with the parent/caregiver and explain that children are often confused about a loved one's death but are afraid to ask questions. Explain that even young children need clarification about what has happened in order to cope and make sense of the loss. If the caregiver feels ready, state that you would like to have a session where the children can freely ask any questions that they might have. Offer support and give a few guidelines. Some of these might include the following.

- Use clear and direct language about death. Do *not* use euphemisms such as "asleep," "lost" or "passed away."

- Be prepared to repeat explanations. Children need repetition in order to understand.

- Be completely honest—even if you don't know the answer, say "I don't know."

- Don't be afraid to show emotion and to let your child know that it is okay for you to be sad, too.

When it is time for a session that includes the children, state again that children are often confused about a loved one's death but are afraid to ask questions. Explain that it is important for them to understand what happened, so they will be taking turns in asking their parent/caregiver whatever questions they have about the circumstances around the loved one's death or the current family situation. If the family needs prompting, the counselor can either ask the caregiver to describe what happened or ask the children what they understand about the death. After all questions have been asked and answered, compliment the family on their openness and courage.

DISCUSSION QUESTIONS

- What was the hardest thing to talk about? What was the easiest?

- Do you think anyone held back when asking questions because they were uncomfortable?

- Sometimes answers create more questions. Do you have any new questions that you would like to ask now or at a later time?

- If, at a later time, you *do* want to ask more questions, who would you ask and when would be a good time to do it?

- When friends and neighbors ask questions, what can you say?

- What has been the most challenging part of your loss so far?

FIB OR FACT?

PARTICIPANTS
Parent/caregiver(s) and children (ages 10–18)

PURPOSE
To educate the family about grief and to dispel any unrealistic expectations about their own grieving process

MATERIALS

- Index cards
- Pen/pencil
- Tape

DESCRIPTION

Prior to the family's arrival, write down the following statements on index cards but do *not* indicate if they are fib or fact. Mix them up and place them in a pile.

FIB (MYTH)

- Staying busy is a good way to cope.
- If someone is not showing her/his emotions that means they are handling grief well.
- Grief is over after the first year.
- If one ignores grief it will go away.
- Everyone grieves in the same way.
- The grieving process happens in an orderly and predictable way.
- The goal of grief is to get over it.

FACT (TRUTH)

- Grief work is about learning how to live with the loss.
- There are several stages of grief with different kinds of feelings.
- People can have grief bursts at unexpected times.
- Grief can make it difficult to concentrate.
- Grief suppresses the immune system.
- Grief can cause spiritual questioning.
- During grief some people see or hear the voice of the deceased.

When the family arrives, explain to them that it is important to understand the grieving process so that they do not feel "crazy." Explain that there are many myths about grief and believing any of them can make grieving more difficult. Ask the oldest family member to turn over the first index card, read the statement and identify if it is a *Fib* or a *Fact*. The counselor should verify whether this is the correct answer. If it is a fib, ask the family member to tear up the card; if it is a fact, they should tape it to the wall. Proceed to the next family member and continue until all the cards have been read and identified.

DISCUSSION QUESTIONS

- Were you surprised by which statements were fibs (myths) and which ones were facts (truths)?
- Which fact were you most relieved by?
- Which facts have you experienced? How has this affected you?

- Were there any fibs that you previously believed? Where do you think those came from? How did they affect you?

- What are some facts about *your* family's grief?

MEMORY BOOK

PARTICIPANTS
Parent/caregiver and children (ages 4–18)

PURPOSE
To remember the deceased loved one in a three-dimensional way and to make meaning of her/his life

MATERIALS

- Scrapbook or photo album

- Pens and/or markers

- Tape

- Craft supplies (i.e. glitter, ribbon, stickers, etc.)

DESCRIPTION
Prior to the session, explain to the family that they will be creating a Memory Book and ask each of them to bring photos and souvenirs from their loved one's life. At the session, encourage them to draw pictures or write down descriptions of specific memories that they have of their loved one. Direct them then to organize these in some way as they assemble and decorate their Memory Book. If families need prompts, some of the following ideas can be used:

- happy memories

- sad memories

- funny memories

- hobbies

- holidays

- work.

DISCUSSION QUESTIONS

- What feelings bubble up for you as you look over your Memory Book? How do you feel about having these emotions? Is it okay to have several feelings at the same time?

- What was the best part about putting this Memory Book together? What was the hardest part?

- What would your loved one say about this Memory Book if s/he were here?

- What will you do with this Memory Book now that it is made?

- Are there memories that you wanted to include but didn't?

- Are there any memories that you purposely didn't include?

- How would you feel about sharing your Memory Book with others?

OUR BROKEN HEART

PARTICIPANTS
Parent/caregiver and children (ages 7–18)

PURPOSE
To recognize individual family members' shared loss, to acknowledge differences in grieving and to inspire hope for healing

MATERIALS

- Paper

- Pens and/or markers

- Tape

DESCRIPTION
Prior to the family's arrival, cut out a large heart from a piece of paper. Tear the heart into the same number of pieces as there are family members so that everyone will receive one piece of the heart. When the family is present, hand each person their piece of the heart and ask them to write down several feelings related to their grief. Then ask the family to put the heart back together (like a puzzle). When the heart has been completely put back together, ask each family member to take a piece of tape and tape one section of the reconstructed heart to another. Ask them to write down a source of support on the piece of tape. Repeat until every family member has had a chance to place tape on the broken heart.

DISCUSSION QUESTIONS

- What feelings do some of you have in common? What feelings are different?

- How is it that your family shares the same "heart?"

- Sometimes families feel ripped apart after a death. Has your family felt like this?

- How can you come together around your shared grief?

- How can you let each other know when you need support?

- Which of these sources of support are you most likely to use?

- How can each family member "bend like a willow but not break like a twig"?

BEREAVEMENT BOARD GAME

PLAYERS
Parent/caregiver and children (ages 6 and up)

PURPOSE
To improve communication and cohesion

MATERIALS

- Snakes and Ladders board game
- Appendix A cards (discussion, interactions and feelings)
- Appendix J cards (bereavement)

DESCRIPTION
Make photocopies of the four sets of game cards (Appendices A and J) using four different colors of copy paper (or simply write "Bereavement," "Discussion," "Interactions" and "Feelings" on the backs of the appropriate cards). Then play Snakes and Ladders (moving up or down the board if you land on a ladder or a snake) with a difference—when players land on a numbered space they must answer a question from one of the four sets of cards. If they land on numbers 1–25 they should answer a "Families in grief" card; if they land on numbers 26–50 they should answer a "Discussion" card; if they land on numbers 51–75 they should answer an "Interactions" card; if they land on numbers 76–100 they should answer a "Feelings'" card. The first player to reach the top wins.

DISCUSSION QUESTIONS

- What did you learn about your family in this game?
- What did you learn about yourself in this game?
- What were the easy questions to answers? What were the hard ones?
- Were there any questions that brought out strong feelings in you? What were they?
- Is there a particular card/question that you would like to talk about more?

BEFORE AND AFTER

PARTICIPANTS
Parent/caregiver and children (ages 5–18)

PURPOSE
To recognize changes in family structure and family roles

MATERIALS

- Paper
- Crayons and/or markers

DESCRIPTION

Provide each family member with two sheets of paper. Direct each family member to draw a picture of their family before the death of their loved one on one sheet and draw a picture of their current family on the other sheet. When everyone has completed their pictures, ask them to share their pictures with the group. Encourage family members to refrain from any criticism or challenging questions.

DISCUSSION QUESTIONS

- Based on everyone's pictures, what are some of the major changes that you see in your family?
- What family members' pictures are similar and what family members' pictures are different?
- Do you see any role changes in your family? If so, how is everyone handling those role changes?
- What are some of the positive things that you see in your second pictures?
- Is there a role in your family that you would *like* to see changed? Why?

THUMB-BALL SUPPORT

PARTICIPANTS

Parent/caregiver and children (ages 7–18)

PURPOSE

To identify individual and family support systems

MATERIALS

- Ball
- Markers

DESCRIPTION

Prior to the family's arrival, purchase a round ball of any type (i.e. soccer ball, volleyball, beach ball, etc.). Write the following sentences all over the ball.

1. Name two people you are comfortable talking to outside of your family.
2. Name someone in your family who you are comfortable talking to when you feel sad.

3. Name a place where you can go that feels safe and calm.

4. Name two things you can do when you are feeling sad.

5. Name two safe things you can do when you are feeling angry.

6. Name two things you can do to feel competent, strong or smart.

7. Name one activity you can do to express your feelings. Examples: writing, drawing, listening to music, playing sports, dance.

8. Name two activities that give you pleasure.

9. Name someone you can ask for a hug from.

10. Name someone who makes you laugh.

11. Name someone you feel comfortable approaching to ask questions about your deceased loved one.

12. Name someone you know who has also had a loved one who died.

13. Name the thing/person that helps you the most as you live with your loss.

14. Name something that you can do to help a family member.

During the session, ask family members to stand in a circle and toss the ball to one another. Each time that a family member catches the ball, instruct her/him to read and answer the statement closest to her/his left thumb. Continue for several rounds.

Variation: You can simply write numbers 1–14 around the ball and have a sheet of paper with the numbered directives. When the family member calls out the number that her/his left thumb is next to, you can read the same numbered instruction.

DISCUSSION QUESTIONS

• What did you learn about your family's support systems?

• Were you surprised about any of your family members' responses?

• Were there any questions that were difficult to answer?

• On a scale of one to ten how open are you personally to asking for and receiving support?

• Has there been anything good in your family that has come from your loss? If so, what?

STUPID THINGS THAT PEOPLE SAY

PARTICIPANTS
Parent/caregiver and children (ages 7–18)

PURPOSE
To acknowledge that not all expressions of sympathy are helpful and to increase family cohesion

MATERIALS

- Index cards
- Pen/pencil

DESCRIPTION

Prior to the family's arrival, on index cards write down inappropriate comments that people make to the bereaved—one statement per card. You can use some of the examples below or come up with some of your own or some that the family has mentioned in previous sessions.

- "Everything happens for a reason."
- "You're not over it yet?"
- "S/he is in a better place."
- "I guess God wants her/him with Him."
- "Guess her/his time was up."
- "Be strong."
- "I don't see how you get out of bed in the morning."
- "I know how you feel."
- "It'll get better."
- "At least you knew it was coming." (If the death was anticipated.)
- "At least s/he didn't suffer." (If the death was sudden.)

When the family arrives, explain that they will be helping each other come up with responses to stupid things that people say to the bereaved. Then place the index cards on a table face down (or place them in a bowl or hat). One at a time, family members should pull out a card and read it. Direct the family to brainstorm two different kinds of responses: a silly response and an assertive response.

DISCUSSION QUESTIONS

- How does it feel to work together on a problem like this?
- Which of the questions have you already heard?
- Are there any that you have heard that weren't mentioned here?
- Which ones bug you the most?
- Are there particular people or groups that tend to say stupid things more than others?
- Do you feel more confident now in handling these kinds of statements?
- Which of the responses that you came up with will you use?

LOSS OF A CHILD: PARENT/CAREGIVER(S) COMMUNICATION

PARTICIPANTS

Parent/caregiver(s)

PURPOSE

To enhance communication between parents and to acknowledge each other's different way of grieving

MATERIALS

- Index cards
- Pen/pencil

DESCRIPTION

Hand each parent a piece of paper and a pen or pencil. Ask them to make two vertical lines down the paper so that the sheet has three columns. At the top of each column direct the parents to write the following headings

- What I Need From My Partner
- What I Think My Partner Needs From Me
- What I Think Our Surviving Children Need From Us

Then direct them to list as many things as they can think of under each heading. When both parents have finished writing, explain that everyone grieves differently and that men and women in particular have different ways of grieving. State that you would expect both of their lists to be very different and that you hope they will listen to each other's lists with an open heart when asked to share. Direct them only to listen when the other is reading and not to interrupt. Then ask them to share with one another what they have written. After both of them have shared, ask the discussion questions listed below and then invite each parent to choose one item from the other's What I Need From My Partner list that they would be willing to do. Then ask them to select two items from the What I Think Our Surviving Children Need From Us (one from each parent's list) that they would be willing to do.

DISCUSSION QUESTIONS

- What feelings bubbled up for you as you listened to your partner read her/his list? Were you able to listen to your partner's lists with empathy or did you feel defensive?
- Were there any items from your partner's What I Need From My Partner list that surprised you? What were they?
- Were there any items from your partner's What I Need From My Partner list that you knew but needed reminding of? What were they?

- How similar and different were your two *What I Need From My Partner* lists? Are you okay with the differences?

- What were your thoughts about your partner's What I Think My Partner Needs From Me list?

- Were there any things that surprised you? Were there any things that caused you to feel understood and connected? What were they?

- How similar and different were your two What I think Our Surviving Children Need From Us lists? How do you think your two lists complement one another?

FACE PAINTING

PARTICIPANTS

One parent/caregiver and one child (ages 4–11)*
*This can be done with two parents/caregivers and two children in the room or can be alternated between parents/caregivers and children so that each child and each parent/caregiver has time together

PURPOSE

To increase nurturing touches and looks between parents and children

MATERIALS

- Face paints

- Paintbrushes

- Paper towels

DESCRIPTION

Direct parent/caregiver and child to paint one another's faces in whatever way they wish. Then ask them to describe what they painted and why.

DISCUSSION QUESTIONS

- What thoughts and feelings bubbled up for you as you were having your face painted?

- What thoughts and feelings bubbled up for you as you were painting your child's/caregiver's face?

- Were you careful and gentle with one another?

- What did you see in each other's eyes as you looked at one another's faces?

- How do you nurture one another at home?

- When are the times that you need nurturing? What are the ways that you like to be nurtured?

Additional Activities That May be Helpful

- It Takes a Village in Chapter 3: Single-Parent Families with an Absent Parent (p.27)

- My Superhero Cape in Chapter 4: Divorced/Separated/Unmarried Families—Both parents available (p.45)

- Gaining Perspective in Chapter 6: Families with Grandparents as Caregivers (p.74)

- Healing our Hearts in Chapter 6: Families with Grandparents as Caregivers (p.77)

- A Strand of Angels in Chapter 9: Families with Parent Substance Abuse (p.125)

- Hide and Seek in Chapter 10: Families with a Mentally Ill Parent (p.145)

- A Bag of Coping in Chapter 10: Families with a Mentally Ill Parent (p.148)

References

Affeck, G. and Tennen, H. (1996) "Construing benefits from adversity: adaptional significance and dispositional underpinnings." *Journal of Personality 64*, 899–922.

Barrera, M., D'Agostino, N.M., Schneiderman, G., Tallett, S., Spencer, L. and Jovcevska, V. (2007) "Patterns of parental bereavement following the loss of a child and related factors." *Omega: The Journal of Death and Dying 55*, 145–167.

Bowlby, J. (1980) *Attachment and Loss: Volume 3. Loss: Sadness and Depression.* New York: Basic Books.

Caserta, M.S. and Lund, D.A. (2007) "Toward the development of an Inventory of Daily Widowed Life: guided by the dual process model of coping with bereavement." *Death Studies 31,* 6, 505–534.

Doka, K.J. (ed.) (1996) "Commentary." In *Living with Grief after Sudden Loss: Suicide, Homicide, Accident, Heart Attack, Stroke.* Bristol, PA: Taylor and Francis.

Gilbert, K. (1996) "We've had the same loss, why don't we have the same grief?: Loss and differential grief in families." *Death Studies 20,* 269–283.

Hall, M. and Irwin, M. (2001) "Physiological Indices of Functioning in Bereavement." In M.S. Stroebe, R.O. Hansson, W. Stroebe and H. Schut (eds) *Handbook of Bereavement Research: Consequences, Coping, and Care.* Washington DC: American Psychological Association.

Kubler-Ross, E. (1973) *On Death and Dying.* Routledge.

Kung, H.C., Hoyert, D.L., Xu, J. and Murphy, S.L. (2008) "Deaths: final data for 2005." *National Vital Statistics Reports 56,* 10. Hyattsville, MD: National Center for Health Statistics.

Linley, P.A. and Joseph, S. (2004) "Positive change following trauma and adversity: a review." *Journal of Traumatic Stress 17,* 11–21.

Melhem, N.M., Moritz, G., Walker, M., Shear, M.K. and Brent, D. (2007) "Phenomenology and correlates of complicated grief in children and adolescents." *Journal of the American Academy of Child and Adolescent Psychiatry 46,* 493–499.

Mikulincer, M. and Shaver, P.R. (2008) "Adult Attachment and Emotion Regulation." In J. Cassidy and P.R. Shaver (eds) *Handbook of Attachment: Theory, Research, and Clinical Applications* (2nd edition). New York: Guilford Press.

Morgan, J.D. (2000) *Meeting the Needs of our Clients Creatively: The Impact of Art and Culture on Caregiving.* Amityville, NY: Baywood Publishing Company.

Murphy, S.A. (2008) "The Loss of a Child: Sudden Death and Extended Illness Perspectives." In M.S. Stroebe, R.O. Hansson, H. Shut and W. Stroebe (eds) *Handbook of Bereavement Research and Practice.* Washington DC: American Psychological Association.

Nadeau, J.W. (2008) "Meaning-Making in Bereaved Families: Assessment, Intervention and Future Research." In M.S. Stroebe, R.O. Hansson, H. Shut and W. Stroebe (eds) *Handbook of Bereavement Research and Practice.* Washington DC: American Psychological Association.

Rosenblatt, P.C. (2000) *Parent Grief: Narratives of Loss and Relationship.* Philadelphia: Brunner/Mazel.

Shapiro, E.R. (2001) "Grief in Interpersonal Perspective: Theories and their Implications." In M.S. Stroebe, R.O. Hansson, W. Stroebe and H. Shut (eds) *Handbook of Bereavement Research: Consequences, Coping, and Care.* Washington DC: American Psychological Association.

Shear, M.K., Boelen, P.A. and Neimeyer, R.A. (2011) "Treating Complicated Grief: Converging Approaches." In R.A. Neimeyer, D.L. Harris, H.R. Winokuer and G. Thordon (eds) *Grief and Bereavement in Contemporary Society: Bridging Research and Practice.* New York: Routledge.

Stroebe, M., Schut, H. and Stroebe, W. (2007) "Health outcomes of bereavement." *Lancet 370,* 1960–1973.

Stroebe, M.S. and Schut, H. (1999) "The Dual Process Model of coping with bereavement: rationale and description." *Death Studies 23,* 197–224.

Stroebe, W. and Schut, H. (2001) "Models of Coping with Bereavement: A Review." In M.S. Stroebe, W.O Hansson, W. Stroebe and H. Schut (eds) *Handbook of Bereavement Research: Consequences, Coping, and Care.* Washington DC: American Psychological Association.

Stroebe, M. and Schut, H. (2008) "The Dual Process Model of Coping with Bereavement: overview and update." *Grief Matters: The Australian Journal of Grief and Bereavement 11,* 1–4.

Tedeschi, R. and Calhoun, L. (2008) "Beyond the concept of recovery: growth and the experience of loss." *Death Studies 32,* 27–39.

Webb, N.B. (2004) "The Impact of Traumatic Stress and Loss on Children and Families." In N.B. Webb (ed.) *Mass Trauma and Violence: Helping Families and Children Cope.* New York: Guildford.

Weiss, R.S. (2008) "The Nature and Causes of Grief." In M.S. Stroebe, W.O Hansson, W. Stroebe and H. Schut (eds) *Handbook of Bereavement Research: Consequences, Coping, and Care.* Washington DC: American Psychological Association.

Wijngaards-de Meij, L., Stroebe, M., Schut, H., Stroebe, W., Van den Bout, J., Van der Heijden, P. and Dijkstra, I. (2008) "Parents grieving the loss of their child: interdependence in coping." *British Journal of Clinical Psychology 47,* 31–42.

Wolchik, S.A., Coxe, S., Tein, J.Y., Sandler, I.N. and Ayers, T.S. (2008) "Six year longitudinal predictors of posttraumatic growth in parentally bereaved adolescents and young adults." *Omega 58,* 107–128.

Znoj, H.J. and Keller, D. (2002) "Mourning parents: considering safeguards and their relation to health." *Death Studies 26,* 545–565.

General Game Cards

Describe a time when you felt **happy** with one or more of your family members.

Feelings

Describe a time when you felt **sad** with one or more of your family members.

Feelings

Describe a time when you felt **angry** with one or more of your family members.

Feelings

Describe a time when you felt **scared** with one or more of your family members.

Feelings

Describe a time when you felt **nervous** with one or more of your family members.

Feelings

Describe a time when you felt **surprised** with one or more of your family members.

Feelings

Describe a time when you felt **silly** with one or more of your family members.

Feelings

Describe a time when you felt **relaxed** with one or more of your family members.

Feelings

Describe a time when you felt **excited** with one or more of your family members.

Feelings

Describe a time when you felt **bored** with one or more of your family members.

Feelings

Describe a time when you felt **confused** with one or more of your family members.

Feelings

Describe a time when you felt **embarrassed** with one or more of your family members.

Feelings

Describe a time when you felt **grumpy** with one or more of your family members.

Feelings

Describe a time when you felt **proud** with one or more of your family members.

Feelings

Describe a time when you felt **cheerful** with one or more of your family members.

Feelings

Describe a time when you felt **worried** with one or more of your family members.

Feelings

Describe a time when you felt **lucky** with one or more of your family members.

Feelings

Describe a time when you felt **careful** with one or more of your family members.

Feelings

Turn to the family member on your right and give her/him a compliment. Interactions	Turn to the family member on your right and describe a happy memory that you had with her/him. Interactions	Turn to the family member on your right and give her/him a hug. Interactions
Turn to the family member on your left and tell her/him that you love her/him. Interactions	Turn to the family member on your left and thank her/him for something s/he has done for you. Interactions	Turn to the family member on your left and tell her/him what you think is her/his best quality. Interactions
Turn to the family member across from you and make up a secret handshake together. Interactions	Turn to the family member across from you and ask, "How do I make your day more enjoyable?" Interactions	Turn to the family member across from you and ask, "What should I do when you're feeling angry?" Interactions

Turn to the family member on your left and give her/him a compliment. Interactions	Turn to the family member on your left and describe a happy memory that you had with her/him. Interactions	Turn to the family member on your left and give her/him a hug. Interactions
Turn to the family member on your right and tell her/him that you love her/him. Interactions	Turn to the family member on your right and thank her/him for something s/he has done for you. Interactions	Turn to the family member on your right and tell her/him what you think is her/his best quality. Interactions
Turn to the family member across from you and try to make her/him laugh. Interactions	Turn to the family member across from you and ask, "What is something I should know about you?" Interactions	Turn to the family member across from you and ask, "What can I do for you when you are stressed?" Interactions

What is a recent mistake you made in your family? What did you learn from it? Discussion	When was the last time you caused someone in your family to feel angry? Did you apologize? Discussion	What do you do to help your family get along better? Discussion
Give yourself a "grade" for how well you listen to your family members. How could you improve? Discussion	What is something you can do to make life easier for one of your family members? Discussion	Why is forgiveness important? Who in your family has forgiven you for something? Discussion
Name each family member and one quality that you have in common with her/him. Discussion	Which extended family members would you like to see more often? Discussion	What is a family ritual (habit) that you enjoy? What is a family ritual (habit) that you don't enjoy? Discussion

Why is it important to have families? Discussion	How can family members get closer? Discussion	What does it mean to have good communication? Discussion
Why is it important to be flexible in a family? Discussion	When was the last time you complimented someone in your family? Do it now. Discussion	Why is it important for adults to be in charge of families? Discussion
What is your favorite family holiday? Why? Discussion	Why is it important to let family members have a time out when they are feeling angry? Discussion	Why is it important to have rules in families? Discussion

Single Parent Cards

Are you ever embarrassed about being a single parent family?

Single parent

Do other people ever ask nosey questions about you being a single-parent family?

Single parent

If your family had a motto, what would it be?

Single parent

Do you know any other single-parent families? Name some of them.

Single parent

Are there other people who could help with homework when your parent is busy?

Single parent

If you could change one thing about your family, what would it be?

Single parent

Are there other single-parent families that your family could do things with? Who are they?

Single parent

Do you have family photos of all of you together? Where are they?

Single parent

How do you feel about parents dating?

Single parent

Name two things your family could do together for fun.

Single parent

What are three things your family could happily discuss at dinner together?

Single parent

Who is someone outside of your family who supports your family in some way?

Single parent

Why is it better for a parent (rather than a child) to make the rules in a family?

Single parent

In what ways does the parent in your family protect the kids in your family?

Single parent

Single parents often feel overwhelmed. What can kids do to help their parent around the house?

Single parent

It's tempting for single parents to share grown-up information with children. How can parents remember not to do this?

Single parent

What would you like your family to know about your needs?

Single parent

How are decisions made in your family? What do you like and not like about this?

Single parent

APPENDIX C
Feelings Thermometers

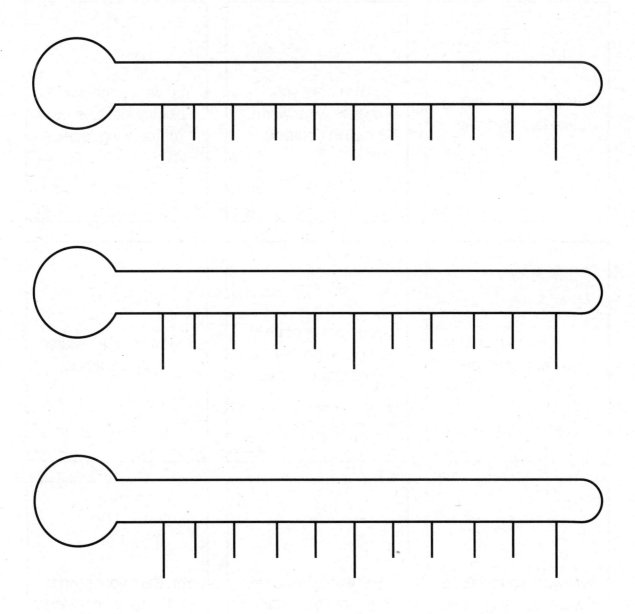

Choice Cards

You want your child to take her medicine. Choice	You want your child to wear warm clothing outside. Choice	You want your child to pick up her toys out of the living room. Choice
You want your child to do her homework. Choice	You want your child to come home at a designated time. Choice	You want your children to stop arguing. Choice
You want your child to fasten her safety belt. Choice	You want your child to shut the door. Choice	You want your child to set the table for dinner. Choice

Assertiveness

"You're stupid if you think that."

"I'll do it! Just get off my back about it."

"If you don't let me play, I'm going to go tear up your homework."

"It's YOUR fault that we don't get along!"

"I'm going to beat the crap out of you!"

"You'd better give me that piece of pie!"

"Shut up!"

"Why are you always so friggin' late?"

"Don't tell me what to do with my own money!"

"I'm not sure I agree but that's an interesting way to look at things."

"I was just in the middle of ending this phone conversation. I'll do it as soon as I get off."

"I would really like to play this game with you. What do you think?"

"We've had a lot of trouble getting along. I think both of us should work on it."

"I'm really angry with you right now."

"I think that was my piece of pie. Would you give it to me please?"

"Would you be quiet please? I'm trying to watch this show."

"I really hate it when you're late. Do you think you could try to be on time?"

"I appreciate your ideas but I have my own thoughts about how to spend my money."

"You must be right."	<Silence>	"Here, you go ahead and play. I don't have to play right now."
"We've had a hard time getting along lately. I'm sure it's all my fault."	"It's nothing. Really."	"You can have it. It's okay. I don't mind if I don't get any pie."
<Stays quiet about having a hard time hearing the TV because others are making noise>	"Sigh."	"Yeah, your ideas are probably better than mine."

Impulse Control

The computer is not working right. You have the impulse to hit it. What might happen?

You and the person on your right are arguing. You have the impulse to call her/ him a rude name. What might happen?

You are trying to get through the doorway and the person on your right is standing there and won't move. You have the impulse to push her/him. What might happen?

You are reading a fabulous book and have the impulse to stay up very late in order to finish it. What might happen?

You are starving and the person on your right has saved a piece of pizza in the refrigerator for later. You have the impulse to eat it. What might happen?

There is a party that you really want to go to but you don't want your other family members to know that you are going. You have the impulse to lie about your whereabouts. What might happen?

The family member on your right just used something of yours without asking. You have the impulse to yell at her/him. What might happen?

The family member on your right just got a new haircut and it doesn't look so great. You have the impulse to make fun of it. What might happen?

You just got a bad report card (speeding ticket if an adult). You have the impulse to hide it. What might happen?

The person on your left got home really late last night. You have the impulse to accuse them of doing inappropriate things. What might happen?

You've had a really bad day and now your family is on your back about all kinds of things. You have the impulse to throw a lamp. What might happen?

The person on your left comes out wearing something of yours without permission. You have the impulse to pull it off them. What might happen?

The person on your left is really upset about something and trying to talk to you about it. You have the impulse to say you have to go and do something else. What might happen?

The person on your left keeps making weird noises. You have the impulse to squeeze her/his arm and say through clenched teeth, "Stop it." What might happen?

The person on your left has been in the bathroom for a really long time. You have the impulse to kick the door. What might happen?

You are playing a game with your family and you think that someone has cheated. You have the impulse to flip over the game board. What might happen?

Your family is at a funeral together. You see something funny and have the impulse to laugh hysterically. What might happen?

You see the person on your left making some not-so-good choices. You have the impulse to give them a big lecture. What might happen?

Values Cards

Creativity Values	Freedom Values	Integrity Values
Ambition Values	Success Values	Honesty Values
Beauty Values	Peace Values	Connection Values

Spirituality Values	Love Values	Health Values
Respect Values	Pleasure Values	Humor Values
Intellect Values	Prosperity Values	Simplicity Values

Nature Values	Cleanliness Values	Order Values
Adventure Values	Solitude Values	Physical fitness Values
Recognition Values	Sensitivity Values	Playfulness Values

Agreeableness Values	Decisiveness Values	Open-mindedness Values
Perseverance Values	Kindness Values	Reasonableness Values
Thrift Values	Trust Values	Power Values

Substance Abuse Cards

What are most of the conflicts about in your family? Substance abuse	What does it mean for someone to be in denial? Substance abuse	What role does spirituality play in your family? Substance abuse
How do you know if your loved one is sober or intoxicated? Substance abuse	Do you feel like you've missed out on anything because of substance abuse in the family? Substance abuse	What do you do to take care of yourself when you're feeling upset? Substance abuse
Do the rules in your family stay the same and get the same consequences all the time? Substance abuse	What is something you would like your family to know about your needs? Substance abuse	What does your family do to have fun together? Substance abuse

| If you could change something in your family, what would it be?

Substance abuse | Do you know what to do in case of danger or an emergency?

Substance abuse | Does drinking/ drug abuse look the same in real life as it does on TV?

Substance abuse |
|---|---|---|
| Do you know other families affected by drugs or alcohol?

Substance abuse | What is AA and Alcoholics Anonymous?

Substance abuse | What is the Serenity Prayer and what does it mean?

Substance abuse |
| Has lying been a problem in your family? What are the consequences of lying?

Substance abuse | What is your favorite memory of a family time together?

Substance abuse | Do you have family members outside of your immediate family who also have problems with drugs or alcohol?

Substance abuse |

Ill Child Cards

What are most of the conflicts about in your family? Ill child	When are the most stressful times in your family? Ill child	Name three facts that you know about <illness>. Ill child
Who in your family worries most about <illness>? Ill child	Who in your family worries least about <illness>? Ill child	What qualities do all the children share or have in common? Ill child
If you could say something to <illness> what would it be? Ill child	Does <illness> stop your family from doing things? What other things could you do instead? Ill child	When kids break rules are the consequences the same for each child? Why or why not? Ill child

What is it like for everyone when it's time to go to the doctors or hospital?

Ill child

Do you know other families who have children with the same diagnosis?

Ill child

What fun activities does your family enjoy doing all together?

Ill child

What are the kids' reactions when parents get stressed out?

Ill child

What is a funny memory that your family has shared?

Ill child

What are the things that stress out your parents the most?

Ill child

Are there things that you would like to ask someone in the family regarding <illness>? What are they?

Ill child

What are two ways your family can save money?

Ill child

Name all the illnesses that family members have had.

Ill child

Bereavement Cards

Who in your family are you most worried about since the death of your loved one? Bereavement	Who in your family can you talk to about the death of your loved one? Bereavement	What is a happy memory and what is an angry memory that you have with your loved one? Bereavement
How did you find out about the death of your loved one? Bereavement	Is it good to cry when you're sad? Why? Bereavement	What are things you can do to comfort yourself when you are feeling sad? Bereavement
If you could talk to your deceased loved one now, what would you want to ask her/him? Bereavement	How have things changed at your house since the death of your loved one? Bereavement	Who can you talk to *outside* of your family regarding the death of your loved one? Bereavement

What time of day is the most difficult for you? Why? Bereavement	Do you have dreams about your deceased loved one? Bereavement	When was the very last time you saw your loved one before s/he died? Bereavement
What do you know about phases of grief? Bereavement	What are some stupid things people have said to you about the death of your loved one? Bereavement	Do you have any of your deceased loved one's possessions? What do you have? Bereavement
What do you miss the most about your deceased loved one? Bereavement	What are the "rules" about crying in your family? Bereavement	If your loved one could be here for a few minutes, what would you want to ask or say to her/him? Bereavement

Subject Index

Author Index